Management of Portfolios

London: TSO

Published by TSO (The Stationery Office) and available from:
Online
www.tsoshop.co.uk

Mail, Telephone, Fax & E-mail
TSO
PO Box 29, Norwich, NR3 1GN
Telephone orders/General enquiries: 0870 600 5522
Fax orders: 0870 600 5533
E-mail: customer.services@tso.co.uk
Textphone 0870 240 3701

TSO@Blackwell and other Accredited Agents

First published 2011

Second impression 2012

ISBN 9780113312948

Printed in the United Kingdom for The Stationery Office

P002499591   c15   09/12

Contents

List of figures

List of tables

Foreword

Portfolio management is a discipline whose time has come. Recent reports from the UK government's capability reviews, as well as from the National Audit Office, have highlighted the importance of improved prioritization of our investment in change. This is not a challenge facing the public sector alone – ensuring successful delivery and realizing the full benefits, in terms of realizing efficiency savings and contribution to strategic objectives, are of relevance across all sectors of the economy and in all jurisdictions.

It is here that portfolio management plays a critical role in facilitating organizational survival and growth – by better coordinating investment in programmes and projects, improving the management of risk, encouraging collaborative working and by providing accurate, timely information that enhances management decision-making, organizations are able to:

- Invest in the 'right' programmes and projects in the context of the current environmental conditions and the organization's strategic objectives.
- Ensure successful delivery in terms of time, quality, budget and, most significantly, benefits realization.

This is particularly important in challenging economic conditions as portfolio management:

- Enables more informed cost cutting by providing a clearer view of priorities and the impact of cuts both in the short and longer term.
- Helps to ensure successful delivery of efficiency initiatives and realization of the required savings.
- Provides a means for greater efficiency in the delivery of change initiatives via improved resource planning, dependency management and streamlined procedures.
- Lays the basis for more informed resource allocation, improved delivery and greater benefits realization going forward.

This guide has been prepared to provide practitioners with the grounding to apply portfolio management within a wide variety of organizations. As such it encompasses consideration of the principles upon which effective portfolio management is based; the key practices, including examples of how they have been applied in real-life situations; and guidance on how to implement portfolio management and sustain progress. I commend it to you.

David Pitchford

Executive director

Major Projects Directorate

Cabinet Office

Acknowledgements

The commissioners and publishers are grateful to the following for their contributions to the planning, design and development of this new Best Management Practice guidance.

Authors

Stephen Jenner   Chair of the APM Portfolio Management Specific Interest Group

Craig Kilford Cansoti.com

Project governance

Mike Acaster Project executive, OGC
Eddie Borup Senior user, BPUG
Janine Eves Senior supplier, TSO
Neil Glover Project manager, TSO
Richard Pharro Senior supplier, APM Group Ltd

Further contributions

A wide range of stakeholders were involved in the design and review of this guidance to ensure that it reflects best practice in this emerging field. Grateful thanks are due to the individuals and their organizations, set out below, for their contributions to the new guide.

Design review

Malcolm Anthony, PWC UK; Tim Banfield, National Audit Office; Nicky Bloomer, ACPO (Terrorism & Allied Matters); Richard Caton, London Borough of Hackney; Tim Ellis, Royal Borough of Kensington and Chelsea; Chris Hobson, Citi Ltd; Darren Hughes, HMP & YOI Reading; David Palmer, Home Office; Mike Pears, Department for Education; Stephen Tatler, HMRC; David Watkinson, Identity and Passport Service (IPS); Andy Woodward, NHS Connecting for Health.

Reviewers

Nicky Bloomer, ACPO (Terrorism & Allied Matters); Kevin Brooks, Treetops Training Ltd; James Butler, Program Framework; Marcus Byrne, NHS Walsall; Richard Caton, London Borough of Hackney; Graham Colborne, Silver Chain, Australia; Arthur Coppens, Getronics Ltd; Terry Dailey, Northamptonshire County Council; Alan Dickinson, The Knowledge Alliance; Tim Ellis, Royal Borough of Kensington and Chelsea; Alan Ferguson, AFA; Chris Ferguson, Novare Consulting Ltd; Dan Fisher, Cambiel; Ross Garland, Ross Garland and Associates; Peter Glynne, Deloitte MCS Ltd; Sarah Harries, Open Reach; David Hinley, Enodatum Ltd; Michael Hougham, GMEC; John Howarth, Tanner James; Piotr Kotelnicki, CRM plc; Kaye Law, Portfolio Office, SOCA; Kevin Ling, SureChange Ltd; Vincent Marsi, HiLogic; Bruce McNaughton, Customer Driven Solutions Ltd; Andy Miller, PWC UK; David Palmer, Home Office; Kevin Parker, UK Sport; Adrian Pyne, ProgM (the APM programme); Paul Rayner, Logica; Tim Reeks, HMRC; Michelle Rowland, A&J Project Management Ltd; Abubaker Sami Ali, Blue Nile Dairy Company, Sudan; Richard Sellwood, Catalyze; Rod Sowden, Aspire; Caroline Stanger, Stanger Consulting Ltd; Jennifer Stapleton, Outperform UK Ltd; Stephen Tatler, HMRC; Andy Taylor, Aquila Business Services Ltd; Dr Bernd Vogel, Henley Business School; Sue Vowler, Project Angels; David Watkinson, Identity and Passport Service (IPS); Phil Wilson, Catenary Solutions; Andy Woodward, NHS Connecting for Health.

Case studies and examples

Tim Carroll (Standard Chartered Bank); Heather Darwin (Peterborough City Council); Victoria Ford (DVLA); Paul Hirst (HMRC); Bob Kitchen (Catalyze); David Palmer (Home Office); Rob Parker (Pcubed).

Executive summary

Programmes and projects have been the focus of organizations' efforts to manage change for many years. More recently, portfolio management has come to the fore as organizations have become increasingly aware that delivery is only half the battle. Just as important is whether or not the change initiatives are the 'right' ones and whether the potential return on investment is achieved. Portfolio management can help with this by ensuring that:

■ The programmes and projects undertaken are prioritized in terms of their contribution to the organization's strategic objectives and overall level of risk.

   This is an active process where programmes and projects are regularly assessed to ensure they are contributing, and will continue to contribute, to the strategic objectives. Portfolio management provides the discipline to ensure that funding and other resources are reallocated appropriately if this is not the case.

■ The portfolio of change initiatives is collectively sufficient to achieve the desired contribution to strategic objectives.

■ Programmes and projects are managed consistently to ensure efficient and effective delivery.

■ Benefits realization is maximized to provide the greatest return (in terms of strategic contribution and efficiency savings) from the investment made.

What is a portfolio and what is portfolio management?

Portfolios represent the totality of an organization's investment (or segment thereof) in the changes required to achieve its strategic objectives. Portfolio management is a coordinated collection of strategic processes and decisions that together enable a more effective balance of organizational change and business as usual. As such, portfolio management provides senior management with reliable evidence enabling better and more informed investment decisions about:

■ Where to invest in new initiatives
■ Whether or not to continue to invest in existing initiatives
■ How to ensure efficient and effective delivery
■ How to maximize the return on investment.

It goes beyond passive monitoring of progress to actively managing the composition and delivery of the portfolio as a whole, as well as ensuring that teams are energized, benefits realization is optimized and that lessons are learned and applied going forward.

This practitioner's guide and the accompanying executive guide are structured around:

■ Five flexible principles upon which successful approaches to portfolio management depend. These are:
   ● Senior management commitment
   ● Alignment with the organization's governance framework
   ● Alignment with the organization's strategic objectives
   ● The use of a portfolio office (virtual or otherwise) to support senior-management decision-making
   ● Working within an energized change culture.
■ Twelve portfolio management practices grouped within two cycles:
   ● The portfolio definition cycle – understand, categorize, prioritize, balance and plan
   ● The portfolio delivery cycle – management control, benefits management, financial management, risk management, stakeholder engagement, organizational governance and resource management.

When these practices are implemented in a way that complements existing organizational governance structures and processes and is underpinned by a collective teamwork culture in which staff work collaboratively in pursuit of shared goals, the result is improved portfolio prioritization, delivery and benefits realization.

These principles and practices are illustrated in Figure 0.1.

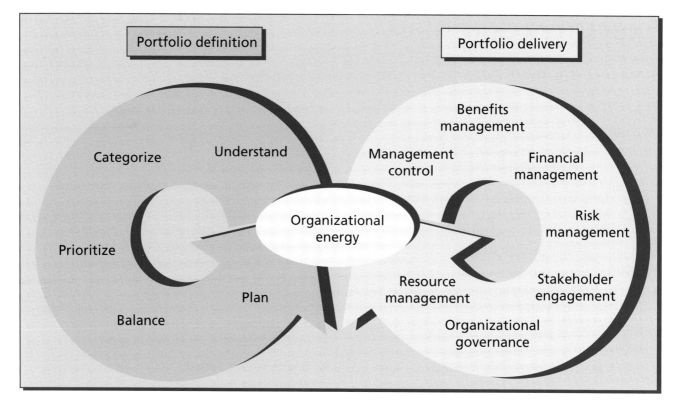

Figure 0.1 The portfolio management cycles

This guide shows that portfolio management is most effective when applied to the organization's investment in change as a whole. Consequently, the focus here is on the organization's collective investment in programmes and projects (or change initiatives) that contribute to the achievement of strategic objectives and business priorities.

While portfolio management will be more effective where robust programme and project management (PPM) exists, this is not a prerequisite for the implementation of portfolio management – questions about strategic alignment, overall capacity and affordability do not need to wait on the achievement of mature levels of delivery capability. Additionally, portfolio management does not replace or seek to micro-manage PPM; rather it seeks to ensure that PPM operates efficiently and effectively at a collective level and is coordinated with strategic, financial and performance management in the interests of the organization as a whole.

It is also important to emphasize that:

■ This does not necessarily mean significant additional spend or bureaucracy – portfolio management should pay its way from:

- Improved coordination of existing functions and processes
- More effective delivery
- More efficient resource management
- Enhanced benefits realization.

■ Additional IT solutions are not a necessary requirement. Such solutions can certainly add value, particularly in large portfolios, but process and governance come first.

■ Sophisticated approaches are not always superior to simpler, 'lite' techniques such as those outlined in this guide (including those that make use of the Pareto or 80:20 rule).

■ Appropriate solutions will ultimately vary from organization to organization, reflecting factors such as their culture, governance and strategic objectives. Scalability is thus a key attribute of effective approaches to portfolio management – applying the principles and 'fit for purpose' practices in a manner that is tailored to the specific local circumstances and existing processes. The examples included in this guide illustrate how organizations have adapted the principles and practices outlined to suit their circumstances.

- Implementation of portfolio management can be effectively handled in a staged or phased manner starting with areas of greatest need, and quick wins (cheap, easy and achievable initiatives) can help demonstrate the value of a portfolio management approach.

Whatever an organization's current level of maturity, this guide will provide advice and insights to assist the design of an appropriate roadmap reflecting accepted good practice and the experience of those who have already successfully adopted portfolio management. The potential benefits are real and significant – research[1] from the public and private sectors, in the UK and abroad, has identified that organizations which adopt a portfolio management approach can realize benefits in terms of:

- More of the 'right' programmes and projects being undertaken
- Removal of redundant, duplicate and poorly performing programmes and projects
- More effective implementation of programmes and projects via consistent approaches and improved dependency management
- More efficient resource utilization
- Better management of risk at a collective level
- Greater benefits realization and return on investment
- Enhanced transparency, accountability and corporate governance
- Improved engagement and communication between senior management and staff.

This last point is significant – portfolio management facilitates collaborative working in pursuit of the organization's strategic objectives. In so doing, portfolio management ensures that limited funds and other constrained resources are allocated to optimize strategic impact and then coordinates delivery and maintains strategic alignment. Finally, portfolio management is concerned with ensuring that the organization realizes the full potential benefits from its investments, and that lessons learned are applied to new investments.

Introduction

1

1 Introduction

1.1 PURPOSE OF THIS CHAPTER

This chapter summarizes the purpose of this guidance, the main areas covered in the subsequent chapters and the target audience.

1.2 PURPOSE OF THIS GUIDANCE

The purpose of this guidance is to provide practitioners with universally applicable principles and practices that will enable individuals and organizations (large or small) to successfully introduce or re-energize portfolio management approaches. Specifically, this guidance provides:

- An overview of portfolio management – what it is, the case for doing it, how it fits with other related organizational activities, how to get started and sustain progress.
- Descriptions of the principles and practices upon which successful approaches to portfolio management are built.
- Examples of portfolio management that illustrate how the principles and practices can be adapted to suit local circumstances.

The portfolio management principles and practices discussed in this guide are presented in such a way that should an organization choose to implement them, it can expect to see real benefits in the short term. Indeed, many organizations have reported that just having an overview of all initiatives, their costs and benefits has provided a basis for making decisions that have enabled more to be delivered from less. Where an organization is already fairly mature in its use of portfolio management (as assessed via a suitable maturity framework such as P3M3® or the health check assessment from the accompanying executive guide that is reproduced in Appendix A), this guidance will assist with the attainment of even more effective and efficient practices.

1.3 STRUCTURE OF THE GUIDANCE

This guide firstly introduces the definition of portfolio management and an overview of the strategic and organizational contexts within which it operates. Following this, the portfolio management principles and practices are discussed in detail. The appendices contain additional useful information. Table 1.1 provides a brief summary of each chapter.

Throughout the guide you will notice the use of 'important notes' (as shown below) and 'keys to success' tables.

Important note

This is used to emphasize a point or to ensure the understanding of a specific element of the discussion.

1.4 TARGET AUDIENCE

The portfolio management principles, cycles and practices described in this guidance are applicable to most organizations irrespective of sector, size (aside from the smallest operations and those with small change portfolios), market or geographical location. Anyone with an interest and/or role in delivering programmes and projects, and organizational strategy from inception to delivery, will benefit from reading this guidance (as shown in Table 1.2). This includes members of management boards and directors of change; senior responsible owners (SROs); portfolio, programme, project, business change and benefits managers; business case writers and project appraisers; and teams from functions including but not limited to finance, information technology (IT), procurement, human relations (HR), strategic planning and performance management.

Table 1.1 Chapter summary

Chapter	Name	Summary
1	Introduction	Introduces the purpose of the guide, the areas covered and the target audience.
2	What is portfolio management?	Introduces the principles, practices and benefits of portfolio management.
3	The strategic and organizational context	Identifies how portfolio management links to business as usual; strategic/business planning; budgeting and resource allocation; project and programme management; performance management; corporate governance; and other functions with a role in relation to achieving strategic objectives.
4	Portfolio management principles	Discusses the five portfolio management principles: senior management commitment; alignment with the organization's governance structure; alignment with the organization's strategic objectives; the use of a portfolio office (real or virtual); and an energized change culture.
5	Portfolio management cycles	Introduction to the two portfolio management cycles: portfolio definition and portfolio delivery; approaches to the implementation of portfolio management; and how to sustain progress.
6	Portfolio definition cycle: practices 1–5	Describes in more detail the five practices within the portfolio definition cycle and examples of how they have been applied in real-life situations: understand, categorize, prioritize, balance and plan.
7	Portfolio delivery cycle: practices 6–12	Outlines in more detail the seven practices within the portfolio delivery cycle and how they have been applied in real-life situations: management control, benefits management, financial management, risk management, stakeholder engagement, organizational governance, and resource management.
Appendices		
A	Portfolio management health check assessment	A questionnaire to help assess current maturity and identify areas where improvement is required.
B	Role descriptions	Descriptions of key portfolio management roles.
C	Programme and project information template	A template illustrating key data that can be collected as part of the 'understand' practice.
D	Benefits management – an example	An example of how benefits management can be applied at a portfolio level.
E	Portfolio-level documentation	An illustration of the purpose and contents of the key portfolio-level documentation.
F	Assessing the impact of portfolio management	Advice on assessing portfolio performance and the impact of portfolio management.
	Glossary	Definitions of key terms.

Table 1.2   Summary of the target audience and the value they can expect from this guide

Target audience	Value
Board members, senior management, departmental heads	The executive summary and the *Executive Guide to Portfolio management* that accompanies this guidance provide a rapid overview of what to expect from portfolio management and the key questions to ask. This guide can then be used to gain a more detailed understanding of areas of particular interest.
Portfolio directors, portfolio office and strategic planning teams	An understanding of the portfolio management principles and practices and how they can contribute to more effective and efficient delivery and achievement of strategic objectives.
SROs, programme managers, programme office teams, business change and benefits managers	An understanding of the relationship between portfolio management and programme management, how programme functions (including management of dependencies, benefits and risks) fit into the wider portfolio framework, and how change initiatives and business as usual (BAU) are linked.
Project managers and project teams	An understanding of the relationship between portfolio management and project delivery and the links to operations and BAU.
Business case writers and project appraisers	How business case writers and project appraisers can be assisted by taking a portfolio-level view, considering both risk/achievability and return/attractiveness, in the context of the organization's existing portfolio of change initiatives.
Operational management	An understanding of the relationship between BAU and change initiatives – and how portfolio management can help achieve organizational objectives and minimize operational disruption during implementation.

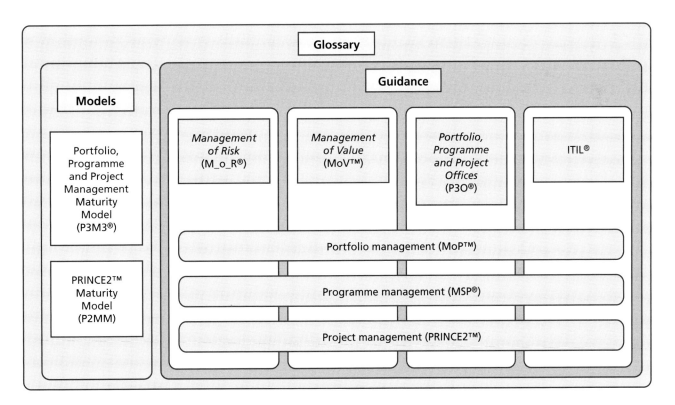

Figure 1.1   MoP's relationship with other Best Management Practice guides

Important note

This guidance is not a 'one size fits all' solution. The principles and practices discussed should be adapted to reflect the specific local conditions including:

- The organizational culture
- Governance structure
- Strategic objectives
- Scale of investment in programmes and projects
- Maturity in programme and project management
- Organizational track record in terms of successful delivery and benefits realization
- Existing strategic planning, financial and risk management processes.

This guidance is a part of, and supports, the OGC's existing selection of Best Management Practice guidance including PRINCE2™, MSP®, P3O® and P3M3. The place of *Management of Portfolios* (MoP)™ within this Best Management Practice guidance is illustrated in Figure 1.1.

What is portfolio management? 2

2 What is portfolio management?

2.1 PURPOSE OF THIS CHAPTER

This chapter introduces the subject of portfolio management and how to get started with implementation. It then provides definitions of portfolio, programme and project management before discussing the key differences between them. Next, it introduces the portfolio management model, principles, cycles and practices, which are discussed in more detail in later chapters. It concludes by considering the benefits of portfolio management and some of the common misconceptions encountered when implementing it.

2.2 BACKGROUND

The success of programmes and projects has historically been gauged by the extent to which implementation has been completed on time within budget and has delivered the required outputs, outcomes and benefits. In many cases, however, organizations have struggled to demonstrate a return on their investment in change, and there is an increasing recognition that true success is only possible if the programme or project was the 'right' initiative to implement in the first place, it actually contributes to the organization's strategic objectives, and the outcome represents value for money. Portfolio management addresses these issues by providing the mechanisms for translating strategic objectives into an appropriate set of programmes and projects (change initiatives), facilitating effective delivery and benefits realization, and capturing and applying lessons learned. As such, the objectives of portfolio management are to ensure that:

- The change initiatives that are being delivered (and those in the development pipeline) represent the optimum allocation of resources in the context of the organization's strategic objectives, available resources and risk or achievability.
- The portfolio is sufficient to achieve the desired contribution to strategic objectives.

- All initiatives are necessary to achieve the desired contribution to strategic objectives.
- The selected change initiatives are delivered effectively and cost-efficiently.
- All the potential benefits are realized.

Experience[2] shows that portfolio management is most effective when applied to the organization's investment in programmes and projects as a whole, which encompasses internal business change, infrastructure and enabling initiatives, as well as improvements in products and customer services. Consequently, the focus in this guidance is on the organization's collective investment in programmes and projects that contribute to the achievement of strategic objectives and business priorities. Nevertheless, improvements will be seen wherever it is applied – at unit, divisional or functional level, although such approaches should be compatible with the organizational-level framework. In this regard, it is noted that whilst the discipline is derived from developments in the financial securities sector[3], much of the practice to date has taken place in the information technology (IT) and new-product development (NPD) fields, although the lessons learned are increasingly being applied in a wider organizational context.

It should also be noted that there is no one right way or 'one size fits all' approach to portfolio management. For example, some organizations will actively manage the allocation of programme and project resources to individual initiatives across the portfolio; on the other hand, there is the model provided by many conglomerates which actively invest and divest in subsidiary companies on the basis of their financial performance but take a less active role in the running of those subsidiaries. Neither approach to portfolio management is 'right' or 'wrong' – it all depends on the circumstances. Ultimately, the principles and practices outlined in this guide should be tailored to reflect the local circumstances, including the organization's culture, governance structure, strategic objectives, maturity in project and programme management, scale of investment, track record in terms of delivery and benefits realization, and existing strategic planning, financial and risk management processes.

Whichever approach is adopted, it does not necessarily mean significant additional spend or bureaucracy – indeed, experience shows that savings are possible from improved coordination, integration and streamlining of existing functions and processes. This is in addition to the value-add that portfolio management can bring from the selection and delivery of change initiatives with greater strategic contribution and savings from earlier termination of lower-priority, non-strategically aligned and poorly performing ones. This point about the cost-effectiveness of portfolio management is reinforced by two further considerations:

■ Portfolio management IT solutions are not a necessary requirement. Yes, such solutions can add value (particularly in large portfolios) by providing a single data repository, streamlining performance reporting and enabling data analysis, but process and governance come first. Many organizations have made significant progress without investing in additional specialized software.

■ Sophisticated approaches are not always superior to simpler, 'lite' techniques such as those outlined in this guide, including:
   ● Driver-based strategic contribution assessment
   ● Three-point estimating and reference class forecasting
   ● Multi-criteria analysis
   ● Decision-conferencing
   ● Staged release of funding
   ● 'One version of the truth' reporting
   ● The champion–challenger model
   ● 'Clear line of sight' planning and reporting (e.g. via investment summary templates and single-page portfolio dashboards)
   ● Management by exception.

A linked point is that implementation of portfolio management can be effectively managed in a staged or phased manner, starting with areas of greatest need, so that quick wins can help demonstrate the value of a portfolio management approach. Thus, whilst this guide outlines a holistic, end-to-end approach to portfolio management, those seeking advice on where to start can learn

from the experience of others. The first steps in a staged implementation commonly include:

1 A crucial first step is to obtain an outline of the organization's portfolio of change initiatives in a single place – including the costs, benefits, schedule, risks and performance to date of all material initiatives (starting with those that consume the most resources). Many organizations have found that just by doing this they have been able to save significant sums of money by removing duplicate, non-strategically aligned and poorly performing initiatives – and in doing so, they have also improved the deliverability of the portfolio as a whole.

2 The next step is often to complete a portfolio delivery plan and to monitor progress against it on a regular basis. Do not wait for perfect information or a fully developed dashboard report – in many cases there will be gaps in the information available, but implementing regular progress reporting will highlight these gaps and stimulate questions and debate.

3 Start tracking completed programme and project performance compared to forecast. Ensure that post-implementation reviews are undertaken and that the results are used to improve business case forecasting. The act of implementing rigorous evaluation will send clear messages that portfolio management means a more disciplined, end-to-end and evidence-based approach to managing change. It will also help ensure more robust and reliable business cases and result in improved investment appraisal and portfolio prioritization.

4 Review the current portfolio and identify dependencies – not only those where one initiative is dependent on the output of another, but also where several initiatives make calls upon a limited resource. Just asking these questions can help to improve understanding across the portfolio and so enable early resolution of potential problems.

5 Establish clear governance structures so that stakeholders understand where decisions are made and the criteria that are used. This helps to ensure that decision makers get the information they require to manage the portfolio.

6 Define a standard set of investment criteria to be used to appraise and prioritize initiatives.

Ensure that these criteria encompass consideration of attractiveness and achievability (just as financial securities are assessed in terms of risk and return) and appraise new initiatives in terms of the incremental impact on the existing portfolio. This helps to ensure that limited resources are allocated with maximum impact.

7 Consider applying staged release of funding linked to stage/phase gates so that investment of resources is associated with confidence in successful delivery. Also, pay particular attention to a rigorous start gate so that programmes and projects are initiated in a controlled manner.

The theme that runs through much of the above is transparency – ensuring there is a clear line of sight on the composition and performance of the portfolio in terms of costs, benefits, schedules, risks and dependencies. Over time, organizations should aim to move to an integrated approach encompassing the twelve portfolio management practices described in this guide, but focusing on the seven areas above will provide a solid foundation for continued improvement and development. Further guidance on implementing portfolio management and sustaining progress is included in Chapter 5.

To emphasize one point, while portfolio management will be more effective where mature approaches to PPM exist, this is not a prerequisite for the implementation of portfolio management; otherwise organizations would need to wait until delivery improves before considering whether they are investing in the 'right' programmes and projects.

2.3 PORTFOLIO MANAGEMENT: DEFINITIONS

It is important to clearly define how portfolios, programmes, projects and BAU fit together to ensure a shared understanding by all stakeholders. The following are the common glossary definitions[4] for portfolio, programme and project management. Links to BAU are described further in Chapter 3.

2.3.1 Portfolio

An organization's portfolio is the totality of its investment (or segment thereof) in the changes required to achieve its strategic objectives. Note

that this does not mean that the portfolio will include all business change, some of which will be delivered via the performance management system (for example, where managers and staff adapt processes or launch low-risk/less complex initiatives to improve performance). Rather, our focus in this guide is on the management of the change initiatives that are delivered via formalized project and programme management methodologies.

2.3.2 Portfolio management

Portfolio management is a coordinated collection of strategic processes and decisions that together enable the most effective balance of organizational change and BAU. Portfolio management achieves this by ensuring that change initiatives are:

- Agreed at the appropriate management level and measurably contribute to strategic objectives and business priorities.
- Prioritized in line with strategic objectives and business priorities and in the context of the existing portfolio, affordability, risk, resource capacity and the ability to absorb change.
- Reviewed regularly in terms of progress, cost, risk, benefits and strategic contribution.

2.3.3 Programme

Managing Successful Programmes (MSP) defines a programme as a temporary, flexible organization created to coordinate, direct and oversee the implementation of a set of related projects and activities in order to deliver outcomes and benefits related to the organization's strategic objectives. A programme is likely to have a life that spans several years.

2.3.4 Programme management

MSP defines programme management as the action of carrying out the coordinated organization, direction and implementation of a dossier of projects and transformation activities (i.e. the programme) to achieve outcomes and realize benefits of strategic importance to the business.

2.3.5 Project

A project is also a temporary organization, usually existing for a much shorter time than a programme, which will deliver one or more outputs in accordance with a specific business case. A particular project may or may not be part of a programme. Whereas programmes deal with outcomes, projects deal with outputs. Further guidance on the management of projects can be found in, for example, PRINCE2.

2.3.6 Project management

Project management is the planning, monitoring and control of all aspects of the project and the motivation of all those involved in it to achieve the project objectives on time and to the specified cost, quality and performance.

From the above it can be seen that the key differences between portfolios and portfolio management on the one hand, and programmes, projects and PPM on the other are:

- Programmes and projects are temporary organizational structures, whereas the portfolio is permanent.
- Programmes and projects are primarily focused on delivery of outcomes/benefits and outputs/products respectively. The portfolio, in contrast, is focused on the overall contribution of these outcomes, benefits and outputs to strategic objectives.
- PPM seeks to ensure successful delivery at the individual programme or project level. Portfolio management is concerned with ensuring that the programmes and projects undertaken are the right ones in the context of the organization's strategic objectives; managing delivery at a collective level; maximizing benefits realization; and ensuring that lessons learned are identified, disseminated and applied in the future.

Important note

Programmes and projects specifically focus on 'doing things right', whereas portfolio management is about a combination of 'doing the right things' and 'doing things right' at a collective level.

2.4 THE PORTFOLIO MANAGEMENT MODEL

2.4.1 The portfolio management model and five principles

Programmes and projects have a start, they have a middle and they will end at some point because they have delivered the outcomes or outputs

they were set up to deliver. To ensure focus, methodologies such as PRINCE2 and MSP contain a number of broadly sequential processes that are used to help deliver successfully – for example, the MSP transformational flow encompasses the following: identifying a programme; defining a programme; managing the tranches; delivering the capability; realizing the benefits and closing a programme. This contrasts with portfolio management, where there is no defined start, middle or end.

The portfolio management model at Figure 2.1 highlights how the portfolio management principles provide the context within which the portfolio definition and portfolio delivery cycles, and their constituent practices, operate. These principles reflect the key foundations on which effective portfolio management is based and are discussed further in Chapter 4.

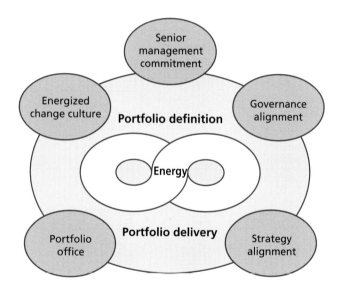

Figure 2.1 The portfolio management model

2.4.2 Portfolio management cycles and practices

Portfolio management activities focus on either defining the portfolio or delivering the portfolio, as illustrated in Figure 0.1.

Chapters 5, 6 and 7 discuss these practices in more detail, but it is important to emphasize that:

- The definition cycle contains a series of broadly sequential practices (i.e. 'understand' generally comes before 'categorize', which usually comes before 'prioritize' etc.) although in practice some overlap will often occur.

- The delivery cycle is different in that the practices here are undertaken broadly simultaneously, but the cycle analogy is still applicable because the individual initiatives go through the programme or project lifecycle, and portfolio delivery is linked to the strategic planning, financial and risk management cycles.

- The definition and delivery practices occur on a continuous basis, although the emphasis accorded to each will vary from time to time – for example, during strategic planning one would expect more emphasis on the portfolio definition cycle.

- The effective operation of these practices will be facilitated by tailored application of the techniques described in this guide. Success also depends on organizational energy – i.e. the extent to which an organization, division or team has mobilized its emotional, cognitive and behavioural potential to pursue its goals.

2.5 THE BENEFITS OF PORTFOLIO MANAGEMENT

Research for the UK Cabinet Office[5] has identified that organizations which adopt a portfolio management approach can realize benefits in terms of:

- More of the 'right' programmes and projects being undertaken in terms of:
  - Greater financial benefits and measurable contribution to strategic objectives.
  - Removal of redundant and duplicate programmes and projects.

- More effective implementation of programmes and projects via management of the project development pipeline, dependencies and constraints (including resources, skills, infrastructure, change appetite etc.) and redirecting resources when programmes and projects do not deliver or are no longer making a sufficient strategic contribution.

- More efficient resource utilization.

- Greater benefits realization via active approaches to exploitation of the capacity and capability created across the organization, and capturing and disseminating lessons learned.

- Enhanced transparency, accountability and corporate governance.

- Improved engagement and communication between relevant stakeholders, including senior managers, in understanding and meeting organizational needs and expectations and in communicating strategic objectives (and the means by which they will be achieved) to all those involved.

To this list can be added improved awareness of aggregated risks; the benefits from senior managers engaging in debate on the contents of the portfolio; improved cross-organizational collaboration in pursuit of shared goals and assurance on consistent and competent programme and project management. This reflects the scope of portfolio management as being to ensure not only that the right initiatives are funded and initiated effectively, but also that these programmes and projects of change are done in the 'right' way.

Example: The benefits of portfolio management

Academic research has identified a significant payback from effective implementation of portfolio management. For example:

- Jeffery and Leliveld[6] at MIT report that those that reach what they term a 'synchronized' level of portfolio management (which they define as resources being actively managed to optimize and balance the portfolio) achieved cost savings of 40%.

- Weill and Ross note that an MIT study of more than 300 enterprises in 23 countries found growth and agility were linked to a portfolio approach.[7]

- The *Harvard Business Review* reported that a pharmaceutical company increased the expected value of its drug development portfolio by around $2.6 bn (25%) without any corresponding increase in spend, via more rigorous prioritization and allocation of available funds.[8]

One other point – in the public sector there are often examples of ministerial mandates being applied, and similar cases arise in the private sector with regard to CEO-favoured projects. This is a fact of organizational life, but portfolio management does ensure in such situations that:

- The impact of pursuing such initiatives, in terms of delaying others, is made clear.
- The rationale for the investment and why the agreed prioritization processes have been by-passed (if they have) are recorded. This often leads managers to ask themselves whether the initiative is such a good idea after all and what further information and assurance may be required concerning the anticipated benefits and how achievability might be improved.

Significantly, portfolio management is relevant in circumstances where cost-cutting as well as revenue growth are the primary strategic imperatives – as is illustrated by the following examples.

Example: Delivering more from less[9]

With public spending under scrutiny, Ashfield District Council looked to portfolio management to help them balance their portfolio of services. They were faced with finding £2.4 m of savings and wanted to achieve buy-in and commitment from the officers and the councillors to the necessary changes.

Rather than implementing budget cuts by distributing them across each department, which can be shown to deliver suboptimal results, a corporate portfolio management approach to zero-based budgeting was employed.

Initially, all activity in each department was taken down to a zero base (only truly mandated activities remained). This enabled the organization to capture everything that they were doing at the time and place them into business-as-usual 'options'. To add to these they then created new change 'options' to enhance services.

By using an open, inclusive, transparent and structured approach to portfolio management all these options were placed into a portfolio and assessed against a handful of criteria to maximize the value the council would achieve from their reduced budget.The resultant portfolio was able to identify a potential 35% increase in value and highlight where improvements in efficiencies were necessary, allowing Ashfield District Council to ultimately deliver more for less. Moreover, the transparent, inclusive, social process ensured that its officers and the councillors were aligned and committed to the corporate plan.

Example: Contributing to enhanced revenue and growth[10]

In 2005, a subsidiary of a global manufacturer had experienced seven years of declining revenue and margins. The newly appointed managing director recognized there needed to be a fresh approach to re-establish profitable growth.

The organization, made up of a number of diverse business units, was undergoing a transition from a division-led to a market-led business model. During this period the head office introduced a cap on headcount (employees), which was a further contributing factor constraining potential growth. With hundreds of existing change initiatives already under way and multiple, often conflicting, objectives, the challenge faced by the incoming managing director was highly complex. The key questions to be answered were:

- Which projects will generate the best return and should therefore be resourced?
- Which projects generate a poor return and should therefore be 'killed' or put on hold?
- What level of investment is needed to fully resource the attractive projects so they can achieve their full potential?
- Which 'core' businesses should release resources to invest in growth projects?

To help answer these questions a new initiative was introduced to implement organization-wide corporate portfolio management. Initially, each business unit created a portfolio of existing projects and new growth projects, using individual business cases that described both the cost and the benefit of each project. A cross-section of stakeholders from the business units used decision-conferencing (see section 6.4.2) to determine the best combination of projects (both existing and new) that would deliver the greatest value for money based on the corporate objectives. These business unit portfolios were then combined into one overall portfolio. A range of stakeholders, representing each of the business units, came together to make the final decision on allocating resources. Their task was to optimize the portfolio and produce a five-year plan.

The portfolio management process was described by the UK board as a planning process which:

- Sets out a clear path for actions and implementation.
- Defines where to invest and the expected returns.
- Lays the foundation for understanding the key risks and challenges.
- Defines and enables agreement to the financial targets that the organization was prepared to commit to.
- Reflects the divisional and regional view of the world.
- Provides a comparative assessment of the market segments and opportunities, and enables realignment of resources where appropriate.

The portfolio management process helped to align resources more effectively with the stated corporate objectives, and through this focused portfolio approach, breakthrough results were obtained. Some of the outcomes achieved at the end of the first 12 months were:

- Fifty existing changes had been stopped.
- Key changes were properly resourced to address the market opportunity.
- An initial reduction in overall headcount, but an increase in headcount for some businesses.
- Growth in sales and margin.
- Better joined-up strategic thinking at global, regional and country levels.

Over the first three years, the achievements included:

- Significant contribution to an increase in shareholder value of $1.2 bn (excluding acquisitions).
- A portfolio management process incorporating all segments, businesses and other (back-office) functions.
- The business earned the right to focus and invest in growth opportunities (global and local).
- Growth and savings discussions created new perspectives and challenged constraints.
- The team was now thinking strategically rather than operationally.

2.6 PORTFOLIO MANAGEMENT – SOME MISCONCEPTIONS

As well as defining portfolio management and its benefits, it is also useful to highlight what it is not, as there are a number of common misconceptions that can cause confusion and detract from successful implementation. **Portfolio management is *not*:**

- **Just another process, system or overhead.** Implementing portfolio management may bring about changes to management board decision-making and the organizational governance processes. It is therefore critical that the person or team leading the development has the necessary skills, credibility and experience (including in relation to behavioural change) and that the management board, together with other key stakeholders, is actively engaged in the development of the portfolio management approach.
- **A group of 'project people' who sit in isolation and produce a plan summarizing what is already scheduled.** Portfolio management is, at least in part, a decision support function and must therefore coordinate its activities with BAU; strategic/business planning; budgeting and resource allocation; project and programme management; performance management; and corporate governance, as well as other functions including IT, HR, finance and commercial. This is considered further in Chapter 3.

Important note

Portfolio management will not make decisions regarding the content of the portfolio, initiatives to be included or to be stopped. It will, however, provide the information that enables senior management to exercise *informed* judgement, and it also makes decision-making more transparent.

- **Programme or project management on a bigger scale.** Programmes and projects focus on implementing change initiatives in the 'right' way; portfolio management is about choosing the initiatives in order to realize benefits that contribute to the agreed strategic objectives (within the constraints of time, cost and capacity) and ensuring the allocation of resources remains optimum in the context of environmental and organizational change. Additionally, whilst portfolio management does not seek to micro-manage programme and project delivery, it is concerned with effective management of dependencies, monitoring progress and taking appropriate action to ensure successful delivery across the portfolio as a whole.

Portfolio management does have some similarities with elements of MSP and PRINCE2 – this is because they provide best management practice processes for planning and delivering change initiatives. Elements of that best management practice are transferable to any situation that requires planning and delivery, including portfolio management. It is for this reason that using elements of MSP and PRINCE2 (e.g. vision, plan, blueprint, programme definition and business case) during the portfolio management definition and delivery cycles will, when used appropriately, add significant value. Additionally, it should be noted that low levels of PPM maturity can compromise the effectiveness of portfolio management via their impact on suboptimal delivery performance – although, as has already been stated, a low level of PPM maturity is not an adequate reason for not implementing portfolio management.

- **Just reporting.** When applied effectively, portfolio management creates a transparent, evidence-based environment that will provide objective and timely information to inform senior management decision-making. Crucially, portfolio management is more than data reporting – it is about providing value-adding information that prompts decision-making. Management by exception (highlighting areas where performance has exceeded a pre-set control limit, either positively or negatively, and may require management intervention) can be an effective way of avoiding swamping the portfolio governance bodies in data and enabling effective decision-making.

- **A rigid, bureaucratic constraint on management decision-making.** Rather, portfolio management is a collection of flexible activities (existing and new) which, when integrated and used collaboratively, enable more effective and informed decision-making. There is no replacement for the exercise of management

judgement, but portfolio management will provide relevant information, such as the investment rationale and progress against plan, that will inform the exercise of that judgement.

- **Just a list of all existing programmes and projects.** Simply creating a list of projects and programmes does not constitute portfolio management. That said, organizations often find real value in a single, complete overview of their portfolio – but the value comes from the action that is taken as a result. The portfolio contains current and planned initiatives that have been prioritized, scheduled and endorsed by the relevant portfolio governance body with costs, benefits, required resources and dependencies identified.

- **A bureaucratic process that prevents or stops programmes or projects for no good reason.** Portfolio management ensures the effective and consistent use of a business change lifecycle, which provides a review of the continued viability and business value of initiatives via regular reporting, stage/phase gates and portfolio-level reviews. In this way it will clearly highlight which programmes or projects are not adding value to strategic objectives (or where delivery is an issue) and will make clear recommendations to the relevant decision-making body. It also enables prompt action to be taken to avoid or address issues that could adversely affect successful delivery. Portfolio management is also **not** about continually stopping programmes and projects in favour of others with a better return on paper – to do so would mean significant wasted expenditure. Rather, it is about ensuring that the portfolio continues to reflect the best use of limited resources in the context of the organization's strategic objectives, and that means that where initiatives do need to be stopped they should be stopped as early as possible.

The strategic and organizational context

3

3 The strategic and organizational context

3.1 PURPOSE OF THIS CHAPTER

This chapter is all about understanding the context in which portfolio management operates and, specifically, the functions with which portfolio management must effectively coordinate its activities in pursuit of strategic objectives. This includes considering the relationship with the following six key functions/activities:

- Business as usual
- Strategic/business planning
- Budgeting and resource allocation
- Programme and project management
- Performance management
- Corporate governance.

These relationships are addressed in turn before a brief consideration of other corporate functions concerned with the achievement of strategic objectives.

3.2 PORTFOLIO MANAGEMENT AND BUSINESS AS USUAL

The relationship between portfolio management and BAU is one that is considered in many organizations when implementing portfolio management. In Figure 3.1 this relationship is represented as a simple concept: 'run the business, change the business'.

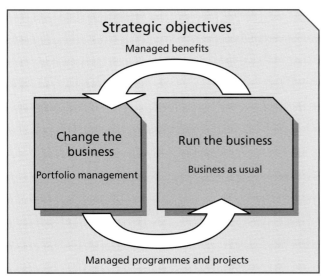

Figure 3.1 'Run the business, change the business'

Figure 3.1 illustrates how portfolio management and BAU combine to realize strategic objectives. Portfolio management controls the major changes to BAU (day-to-day, tactical improvements can be delivered via the performance management system). When change initiatives are successfully implemented, benefits are then realized and operational performance improves. It is this cyclical relationship between portfolio management and BAU that helps achieve the organization's strategic objectives. Yet the reality is that in many cases, organizations struggle to integrate BAU and change initiatives effectively – not least because the focus of business managers and staff can be on today's challenges, rather than on how change initiatives will help them meet these challenges in the future. Portfolio management can make the contribution of change initiatives to operational performance clearer to everyone involved – and not just the forecast impact, but also when this impact will be seen and what metrics will be used to assess it.

3.3 PORTFOLIO MANAGEMENT AND STRATEGIC AND BUSINESS PLANNING

Portfolio management does not try to replace strategic and business planning – rather, it seeks to ensure that the organization's change initiatives represent the optimum allocation of limited resources in the context of the organization's strategic objectives, and that this is maintained in the light of changing environmental conditions. Strategic planning therefore sets the context within which portfolio management operates by providing:

- The basis for determining the scope of the portfolio and the prioritization of individual initiatives. As part of strategic planning, portfolio management addresses four fundamental questions:
  - Are the programmes and projects in our portfolio *necessary* in the context of our strategic objectives?
  - Is our portfolio, together with BAU activities, *sufficient* to achieve our strategic objectives?

- Is the overall level of risk acceptable and is the portfolio of initiatives *achievable*?
- Is the portfolio *affordable* – and if not, which initiatives should be dropped or re-scheduled?

■ The measure against which portfolio management will ultimately be assessed, i.e. whether or not the changes to the business have helped the organization achieve its strategic objectives.

This relationship between strategic planning and portfolio management is, however, two-way. Whilst the former provides the context within which the latter operates, portfolio management also provides information on the contribution that programmes and projects are making to the strategic objectives, and can also lead to a change in strategy, based on achievement of unplanned benefits or failure to realize planned benefits. Furthermore, portfolio management can generate momentum and energy for strategy development: once an organization is confident that it can align its resources and deliver effectively, belief in the value of strategic planning will be enhanced. Guidance on how to align initiatives with strategic objectives is contained in Chapter 4.

An overview of the relationship between strategic planning and portfolio management is illustrated in Figure 3.2.

3.4 PORTFOLIO MANAGEMENT AND BUDGETING AND RESOURCE ALLOCATION

Strategy is little more than intent until it is backed up by the allocation of resources (money, people, equipment, facilities etc.) and portfolio management provides the means by which the link between strategy and resource allocation can be maintained. Resource management in relation to staff, equipment and facilities is covered in more detail in section 7.8 – here the focus is on financial budgeting and the relationship with portfolio management.

Various approaches to budgeting can be adopted in practice. For example, many organizations have devolved budgets with managers controlling the budget for all BAU and change initiatives within their directorate, division or strategic business unit. In such circumstances, portfolio management can be applied within each area, although common standards may be applied across the organization.

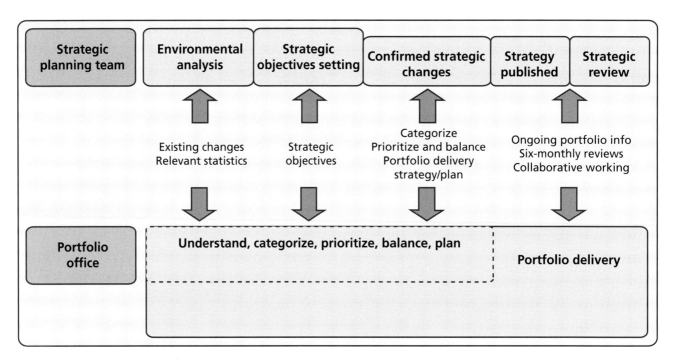

Figure 3.2 Strategic planning and portfolio management

Other organizations have adopted an approach whereby initiatives over a certain value are subject to some central portfolio governance, while the budget for change initiatives remains within operational control. One variation of this approach is where portfolio management is used to coordinate change initiatives that are cross-organizational in scope and benefits.

Another approach is where the budget for programmes and projects, potentially all but often those over a set level, is separated from operational budgets and is controlled by a central portfolio governance body. Here funds are only allocated to initiatives at the point of an agreed business case, and these allocations are then subject to ongoing assessments of viability (via stage/phase gates and regular portfolio-level review) and approval. This is potentially an extremely powerful approach, although it can be challenging to establish given perceptions of its impact on individual managers' autonomy. Where such fears can be overcome, the benefits are potentially great from more effective joint working in pursuit of shared goals. Further information on portfolio financial management is contained in section 7.4.

3.5 PORTFOLIO MANAGEMENT AND PROGRAMME AND PROJECT MANAGEMENT

Whilst programme and project management (PPM) are mechanisms for delivering change, portfolio management encompasses:

- The development of delivery capability organization-wide, via fit-for-purpose standards, processes, and staff development.
- Management of these change initiatives at a collective level including:
  - The management of limited resources such as skilled project managers and other scarce resources (IT architects, finance, commercial and procurement specialists etc.) and ensuring that where there is any shortage they are assigned to the highest-priority initiatives and/or effective action is taken to increase the supply of these resources.
  - Overall risk management, including over-reliance on a single supplier and the risks of cost escalation and benefits shortfalls.

- Dependency management, ensuring that key dependencies are effectively managed across the portfolio.

This also means that project scheduling may be optimal at the project level, but suboptimal at the portfolio level; i.e. a project may well be slowed or speeded up to benefit the portfolio as a whole.

3.6 PORTFOLIO MANAGEMENT AND PERFORMANCE MANAGEMENT

Portfolio management should align with the organization's performance management system. This encompasses:

- Utilizing the expertise of the organization's performance management function in designing and implementing new portfolio performance metrics and driver-based models linking change initiatives, and their benefits, to the organization's strategic objectives (see section 4.5).
- Ensuring that the performance management function is engaged at an early point in the development of business cases and that it validates claimed impacts on organizational performance in the context of the planned impact of the existing portfolio.
- Incorporating the anticipated impact of the portfolio on strategic objectives in the organization's performance targets.
- Making appropriate use of the existing management information system in designing the content and format of portfolio reporting.
- Aligning performance and portfolio reporting, in terms of both timing and content, to ensure consistent messages and effective decision-making.

Portfolio management can also imply changes to the performance management system – in the way individual performance targets are framed on organizational rather than silo-based objectives, and in embedding new behaviours. More information on portfolio performance management is contained in section 7.2 and Appendix F.

Table 3.1 Description of collaborative working between the portfolio office and key departments/ functions

Management board	The portfolio office needed to engage with the members of the management board, both individually and as a team. The management board's involvement was critical as it ensured that the new ways of working were supported from the very top of the organization, which led to departments understanding that this was a serious change. The board also approved the communications that were published to the organization.
	It was also important to ensure that the management board understood how they were going to be involved with portfolio management before it was implemented. Once they were satisfied that the portfolio office would provide them with relevant and reliable information, portfolio management became a specific agenda item at board meetings. This ensured progress was understood and collective decisions were made.
Finance	When portfolio management was first being implemented, the portfolio office did not have the required financial skills, so collaborative working with the finance department was critical in relation to: ■ Determining consistent financial guidance for business case preparation. ■ Developing the annual portfolio financial plan showing the profiled budget. ■ Tracking spend in year. ■ Ensuring the realization of financial benefits by adjusting budgets where appropriate.
Information technology (IT)	A key challenge for the portfolio was to ensure that technology-enabled change initiatives were resourced appropriately. This was only achieved by working closely with the IT programme office to ensure that resources were prioritized in line with the organizational portfolio priorities and that the mechanism to start technology initiatives was aligned with the wider business change lifecycle. It was also crucial that action was taken to manage down the percentage of the IT spend on infrastructure as this enabled more resources to be directed to business value-enhancing initiatives without increasing the overall budget.
Procurement/commercial	A significant proportion of the organization's change initiatives require procurement and commercial advice in order to follow mandated procurement processes. An investment board existed and was integrated into the new portfolio management governance framework. This ensured that key personnel, such as the commercial director, had early sight of proposed new initiatives. This also facilitated early commercial input to business case development, so ensuring more reliable scheduling to realistic commercial timescales.
Strategic planning	During the process of creating the organizational strategy, the strategic planning team worked closely with the portfolio office, primarily because they had access to the most up-to-date information on current and planned change initiatives and understood how they would contribute to the strategic objectives. This was then reflected in the annual plan which the strategic planning team produced.
	More recently, the strategic planning function and portfolio office have participated in horizon-scanning exercises to assess emerging opportunities and ensure these are reflected adequately in the portfolio development pipeline.
Performance management	Without the expertise of the performance management function, the portfolio office would have struggled to identify how each of the change initiatives added value to the overall organizational performance measures. The performance team also benefited from working with the portfolio office because they were able to integrate the information from the portfolio into the organization's balanced scorecard – in this way initiative benefits were linked to the BAU key performance indicators (KPIs). The fact that they now have sight of initiatives from the start means they have a more complete picture when planning the overall target levels of organizational performance.
	Additionally, business case writers now consider the impact on performance from day one – and discuss this with performance management colleagues, resulting in more business-led initiative planning and reliable business cases. In several instances, potential initiatives have been cancelled at an early stage as it has become apparent that no significant operational performance impact was likely.

PPM community	Close working between the portfolio office and the programme and project management community is crucial. The portfolio office provides:
	■ The standards for delivering programmes and projects (including business case and reporting templates).
	■ Assistance with initiative planning and scheduling.
	■ Portfolio dependency workshops.
	■ Help with preparations for stage/phase gate reviews.
	From a portfolio management perspective, strong relationships with programme and project managers are essential, particularly with regard to open and honest reporting on progress. This was helped because the programmes and projects knew that the portfolio office was in a position to facilitate resolution of issues by the relevant portfolio governance body, whereas historically there was nowhere to escalate such issues.
Human relations (HR)	Business change initiatives will almost always impact the structures and working practices of staff. The portfolio office now engages at an early stage with the HR team so they have a view of the anticipated impact of the change initiatives on staff. This is then fed into workforce planning. Close working between HR and the portfolio office has also been of value in ensuring that training is focused on contributing to a closer match between resource demand and supply. Consequently, increased training investment has been justified on the basis of a reduced reliance on bought-in skills.
Business architecture planning	The business architecture team (sometimes called the design authority and situated in the strategic planning, finance or IT departments) manages the overall organizational blueprint (sometimes referred to as the future or target operating model). This defines the current and future organizational design in terms of working practices and processes, information requirements and the technology that supports its operations. Because each of the programmes created a blueprint during initiation, it was possible to align them with the organizational blueprint. The business architecture team was involved in creating the programme blueprints and assisted with the analysis of proposed modifications via the change control process. This team also played a valuable role in providing the mechanism for assessing the net business impact of change initiatives – which informed portfolio scheduling.
Centre of excellence	The centre of excellence (CoE) formed part of the portfolio office and was involved in the design and implementation of the business change lifecycle, supporting standards and templates and training staff so that everyone understood the system and what was required of them. The CoE was also involved in resource capacity planning due to its responsibility for training across the portfolio – which has helped reduce reliance on contractors and consultants.
Real estate and property services	The optimal real estate flexes with the shape and functions of the organization. Major changes to staff numbers (up or down) or to working practices require changes to the property estate. Equally, there are opportunities in terms of relocation to other areas, which help maximize the use and availability of staff and other resources.
Communications	Close working between the portfolio office and corporate communications was required to:
	■ Ensure management and staff had a clear and consistent understanding of the organizational strategy and their role in delivering it.
	■ Engage staff in considering how best to implement the changed ways of working.
	■ Improve the ability of management and staff to make aligned and consistent decisions.
	■ Improve understanding of decisions made elsewhere in the organization.
	■ Ensure consistency in messages.
	■ Facilitate effective ongoing staff engagement.

3.7 PORTFOLIO MANAGEMENT AND CORPORATE GOVERNANCE

Corporate governance is defined as the ongoing activity of maintaining a sound system of internal control by which the directors and officers of an organization ensure that effective management systems, including financial monitoring and control systems, have been put in place to protect the assets, earning capacity and reputation of the organization. Portfolio management supports effective corporate governance because it:

- Links delivery of the organization's strategic objectives with investment in change – and in a demonstrable and transparent way that enhances effective accountability.
- Provides a framework of rules and practices for managing the delivery of the portfolio (and the programmes and projects therein) that are consistent with best management practice.
- Provides clarity on progress against plan.
- Provides a basis for integrated assurance.
- Clarifies responsibility and accountability for making decisions on which programmes and projects will be funded and on what basis – including where and when such decisions are made.
- Provides an audit trail demonstrating the rationale behind investment decisions.

For more information see sections 4.4 and 7.7.

3.8 PORTFOLIO MANAGEMENT AND CORPORATE FUNCTIONS

The implementation of portfolio management can be the catalyst for more effective engagement between corporate functions and change initiatives as all involved can see the contribution to improved performance and their role in supporting this. Table 3.1 contains a selection of extracts from conversations with people (including those in the activities/functions mentioned above) describing how their work links to that of the portfolio office within their organizations.

Portfolio management principles

4

4 Portfolio management principles

4.1 PURPOSE OF THIS CHAPTER

Chapter 2 introduced the subject of portfolio management and Chapter 3 covered the strategic and organizational contexts within which it operates. This chapter begins to explore the detail of how portfolio management works by describing the five principles upon which it is based.

4.2 INTRODUCING THE PORTFOLIO MANAGEMENT PRINCIPLES

The portfolio management principles represent the foundations upon which effective portfolio management is built; they provide the organizational environment in which the portfolio definition and delivery practices can operate effectively. These are generic principles – the way in which they are applied must be tailored to suit the organizational circumstances whilst ensuring that the underlying rationale is maintained.

With this in mind, rather than creating an unrealistic 'to-do list' for each principle or seeking to be too prescriptive, this chapter describes each principle in high-level terms and then outlines a 'target situation' for each, based on good practice derived from organizations that have experience of implementing elements of the relevant principle.

From each 'target situation' it is possible to extract the 'keys to success'. These can be used as a quick checklist to begin to assess the current position of organizations and to inform plans to improve performance. They are given as Tables 4.1–4.5 in the five following sections.

The portfolio model and five portfolio management principles are shown in Figure 2.1.

> **Important note**
>
> The 'target situations' described in this chapter are examples of real-life situations from a number of public and private sector organizations. They are included here as examples to inform understanding.

4.3 PORTFOLIO MANAGEMENT PRINCIPLE 1: SENIOR MANAGEMENT COMMITMENT

Proactive and visible senior management commitment is identified again and again in academic and industry research as being absolutely essential to effective portfolio management. The National Audit Office (NAO)[11] reports that senior-level engagement is crucial in three ways by:

- Providing a mechanism to prioritize the programme and project portfolio in line with business objectives.
- Creating a clear decision-making structure with agreed lines of accountability so that decisions are made swiftly and in line with business strategy.
- Demonstrating that senior management is committed to the change.

Senior managers should support portfolio management in the following ways:

- Publicly championing and positively communicating the value of portfolio management within their areas of command – particularly when the going gets tough and the circumstances demand it as, for example, when an initiative is terminated.
- Participating in decision-making about the composition of the portfolio in a personal, active and positive way.
- Contributing their expertise to the development of portfolio management across the organization.
- Taking effective steps to ensure compliance with portfolio governance and prevent pet projects from being progressed under the portfolio 'radar'.
- Explaining the rationale for decisions to their staff.
- Personally demonstrating the behaviours essential to the success of portfolio management – senior managers must actually do what they say in taking a portfolio-wide rather than departmental perspective.

The target situation

The commitment from our management board was critical in the adoption of portfolio management within the organization. Once the management board received the report defining the current position of all the change initiatives and highlighting the fact that many could not be aligned to our strategy, they understood that portfolio management was needed to ensure that the initiatives were not only delivered successfully, but also that the 'right' initiatives were implemented. The management board recognized there was a strong need for enhanced collaborative working and a standard way to manage change initiatives if they were to make informed decisions.

It was the business change director who ensured that the management board agreed to establish a portfolio office. The management board subsequently endorsed the use of our own standard business change lifecycle, which every programme and project now adheres to, and were engaged as the key decision makers in the categorization and prioritization of all the initiatives within the portfolio. This prompted some lively discussions, one of which led to a management board decision to stop three projects. This had never happened before.

As part of the business change lifecycle, the management board now make the decision on whether or not new change initiatives can start. They actually welcome this involvement because it enhances their control. If an initiative is approved, it is added to the portfolio and included in the monthly portfolio dashboard report that provides key information on portfolio-level progress, risks and issues, and recommendations for any required management board decisions.

The portfolio dashboard is created by the portfolio office, which works closely with all programmes, projects and key departments. This includes the communications section, which in conjunction with the portfolio office ensures that regular and consistent messages are issued with the management board's support. This helps people to see leadership and direction from the top of the organization.

Furthermore, because of this collaborative working, when an initiative attracts a 'red' status (requiring immediate action), it is not viewed as a personal failing any more, but is seen more as something that requires teamwork to resolve. When this happens, everyone works together to bring it back on track or to reallocate resources if necessary.

Table 4.1 Senior management commitment: keys to success

Key	Explanation
A senior management champion	A management board member – for example, the business change or portfolio director (sometimes called the transformation director) or equivalent – must champion the implementation of portfolio management. In other cases this role can fall to the director of strategy or finance director. Whoever it is, they must actually do what they say in demonstrating personal commitment to the portfolio approach.
Clearly defined roles, responsibilities and accountabilities	The roles of the management board and other key positions with regard to portfolio management should be clearly defined and understood. Management should specify all decision points and accountabilities (including those of the management board itself) and portfolio governance should be built into the wider organizational governance framework.
Active engagement	The management board (or sub-board if portfolio functions are delegated) must make decisions regarding prioritization of change initiatives within the portfolio, and subsequently decide what action is required in response to shifts in business priorities and slippage on initiatives. This is turn requires that they are actively engaged in the process – using decision-conferencing techniques (see section 6.4.2) can be very effective in this regard.
A compelling vision	The portfolio strategy should include a compelling vision for the portfolio so that senior managers can see how it relates to the organization's strategic objectives.
Alignment with the reward and recognition strategies	New ways of working and required behaviours should be reflected in the organization's reward and recognition strategies – including senior managers' personal objectives.

4.4 PORTFOLIO MANAGEMENT PRINCIPLE 2: GOVERNANCE ALIGNMENT

Research and practical experience indicate that a key factor behind successful implementation of portfolio management is effective governance, i.e. clarity about what decisions are made, where and by whom, and what criteria are used in reaching these decisions (see section 7.7). This research includes that undertaken for the US CIO Council[12] which notes, 'Large private organizations such as GE Global eXchange Services, Oracle and Lockheed Martin noted that having a governance structure that is well documented, effectively communicated and understood throughout an organization is critical in implementing portfolio management.'

Effective portfolio governance also means that the governance of the portfolio needs to reflect, and be consistent with, the wider organizational governance model; e.g. does the organization have a single governance framework or is a federated structure in place or some form of holding/subsidiary company structure? Developing portfolio management in federated organizations is often problematic if it seeks to extend beyond the component organization boundaries – but a staged, high-level approach can bring real value not least by introducing transparency to the scale and extent of cross-organizational change. The discussion in Chapter 3 on budgeting and resource allocation (see section 3.4) is also of relevance here.

Portfolio management decision-making should therefore be aligned with, and reflect, the wider organizational governance structure. This usually means that decisions about inclusion in the portfolio and responsibility for oversight of portfolio progress lie respectively with a portfolio direction group (PDG)/investment committee and portfolio progress group(PPG)/change delivery committee (with potentially separate committees in each part of the

Example: Portfolio governance[13]

HM Revenue and Customs (HMRC) recognized the importance of separating the governance around portfolio content from that of overseeing and supporting the delivery of the portfolio and its agreed benefits. This ensures that no vested interests are protected in the independent monitoring and decision-making around the progress and continued viability of the portfolio and its constituent programmes and projects.

To underpin this approach, HMRC created an investment committee to make portfolio investment decisions, and a change delivery committee to monitor and assure delivery confidence. Each of these is chaired by a director general and includes director-level members, who can only sit on one committee. Formal links are maintained between the two committees by mandatory shared updates, drafted by chairs after each meeting. Additionally, each chair writes a post-meeting report to the CEO for executive committee discussion.

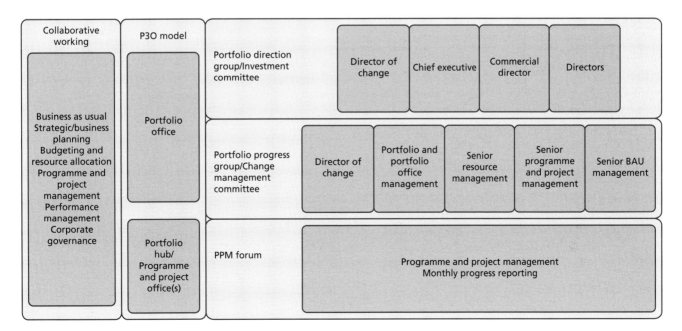

Figure 4.1 Example of a portfolio governance structure

business or for each portfolio segment (see section 6.3) reporting to the main board. In some organizations these boards/committees are combined into a single decision-making body (a portfolio board) reporting to the management board. In others, the management board itself takes this role.

Whether a single- or two-board structure is adopted, the board/committees need to be supported by a portfolio office (this may be a virtual or formal function) charged with establishing, operating and developing the portfolio management processes and information reporting (see section 4.6).

4.4.1 Portfolio governance structure

Based on the target situation described at the end of this section, an example of portfolio management governance structure is outlined in Figure 4.1.

The business change (or portfolio) director, assisted by the portfolio office, should lead on the design and implementation of the portfolio governance structure and ensure that the relevant processes are implemented successfully. This will ensure that the right portfolio information gets to the right stakeholders and at the right time, enabling them to make effective decisions.

Example role descriptions for the PDG/investment committee and PPG/change delivery committee, as well as for the business change/portfolio director,

Important note

The naming conventions of 'portfolio direction group/investment committee' and 'portfolio progress group/change delivery committee' are used in this guide for consistency only and organizations should not feel restricted to using these in their own portfolio management structures. Equally, although the suggested roles in Appendix B are not mandated, the logic should be followed. A management board member champions portfolio management; there should be a board/committee structure for deciding what initiatives are included in the portfolio and for monitoring progress; and some form of portfolio manager role and portfolio office should exist to coordinate the portfolio management operations on a day-to-day basis.

portfolio manager and portfolio benefits manager, can be found in Appendix B. All other role descriptions (or variations thereof) can be found within P3O, MSP or PRINCE2 and are therefore not included in this guidance.

4.4.2 Other important considerations

4.4.2.1 Existing governance structures

There will no doubt be other boards in existence that manage specific elements of the organization, such as a performance management board, an organizational risk management board and perhaps a capital investment board. It is important that these be considered as part of the portfolio governance design – with potentially some rationalization of the board structures. The relationship between portfolio management boards and other relevant boards should be documented in the portfolio management framework so that everyone is clear about who is responsible and accountable for what and to whom.

4.4.2.2 Multi-level portfolios

Some organizations may require more complex portfolio governance structures, particularly in cases where the hierarchy of change has many levels or a number of organizations are working together. For example, some organizations have more than just portfolios, programmes and projects; there could be an organization-level portfolio, a portfolio for each department (such as IT, HR, marketing, commercial and estates etc.), workstreams within those portfolios and programmes, and projects within them. In addition, some organizations use other terminology such as 'strands' or 'super programmes'.

While it is important to ensure that people understand the naming conventions for the multiple levels, role accountability and clarity of board/committee decision rights, the structures must be supported by clearly defined rules for delegation (which may be aligned with budgetary accountabilities), reporting, and escalation of issues for resolution. It is also important that sub-portfolios are reviewed to ensure that investment decisions are optimal not only at the sub-portfolio/

departmental level, but also at the organizational or corporate portfolio level. So-called 'parent' and 'grandparent' portfolio reviews can be useful in this regard, as is an effective portfolio office that can add value by monitoring consistent portfolio definition and delivery across the organization.

4.4.2.3 Should every change initiative be included in the organizational portfolio?

A linked question concerns whether to include all change initiatives in the organizational portfolio. The advantage of this method is that it provides an overview of all change initiatives which can be aligned to the organization's strategic objectives. It also provides an opportunity to understand the entire resource requirements. However, the full value of this will only be realized if the organization is doing some sort of corporate-level capacity planning. More significantly, this approach runs the risk of overwhelming the portfolio governance body with data on change initiatives. Because of this, many organizations only include some initiatives in the organizational portfolio. They can be restricted to those that:

■ Make a material contribution to the organization's strategic objectives
■ Are above a cost threshold
■ Are above a risk threshold.

In such cases there need to be effective checks, in addition to those mentioned above, to ensure sub-portfolios are consistent with the organizational-level portfolio and that initiatives are not deliberately disaggregated into smaller initiatives to avoid portfolio governance. Similarly, when evaluating resource requirements and the business change impact, the portfolio office needs to consider the impact of *all* change initiatives, not just those included in the organizational-level portfolio.

Important note

The example governance provided in this section is relatively simple. There are other important considerations to be borne in mind when designing a portfolio governance structure that will be dependent on the organization's structure, culture, decision-making abilities and current maturity in terms of delivering change.

The target situation

A perception once existed that PPM people deal with the programmes and projects while the rest of us deal with the real business. This was due in part to the management board not being provided with a clear description of all the change initiatives across the organization. Furthermore, there was no single management board member responsible for managing the organization's change initiatives. The CEO recognized that this could not continue – our track record in terms of programme and project delivery and benefits realization demanded a new approach.

A business change director was consequently employed, with responsibility for implementing portfolio management across the organization. A portfolio progress group (change delivery committee) was set up to oversee the implementation, with the business change director as the chair. The portfolio progress group consisted of heads of departments (including business operations, sales and corporate functions such as IT, procurement and HR) and the SROs of the key change initiatives. Although it was useful for the relevant managers to meet and discuss detailed progress, after a while it became clear that although the portfolio progress group had the expertise to make recommendations, key decisions relating to project initiation and recovery actions needed to take place at management board level.

With this in mind, and without wanting to set up a new management board, the business change director obtained agreement to add a one-hour agenda item to the existing monthly strategy day meeting (attended by all management board members) which was called the portfolio direction group. Note – it was subsequently decided to 'split' the meeting timetable with one session focusing on business as usual and the next on the portfolio. This allowed the directors to have quality time to consider the portfolio and debate issues that needed their help to progress and resolve.

During this agenda item, the management board were briefed using the portfolio dashboard. This was received very well because it summarized progress and clearly defined the top issues and risks that needed addressing. It was also designed to reflect what senior management needed to see and to reflect lessons learned.

Once the business change lifecycle was agreed, the management board became involved at key decision points. The portfolio progress group continued but with a modified remit to review all new change initiatives in the context of the current portfolio and make recommendations to the portfolio direction group, in addition to retaining its role in monitoring portfolio delivery. Because the portfolio direction group discussions took place during the existing management board meeting, information was cascaded down via other key organizational boards, such as the finance board or the IT board, which enhanced joined-up communications and enabled more collaborative working.

The portfolio office also set up the portfolio PPM forum – a monthly meeting attended by key senior programme and project managers to discuss progress and key issues. This was a particularly useful communication mechanism for everyone that attended.

Finally, the portfolio progress group meeting was moved to precede the portfolio direction group, which gave the latter access to the most recent progress information as well as the ability to address escalations from the portfolio progress group relatively quickly.

4.5 PORTFOLIO MANAGEMENT PRINCIPLE 3: STRATEGY ALIGNMENT

This is important because the ultimate objective of portfolio management is to facilitate the achievement of strategic objectives. Strategic alignment means that the allocation of funds to different types of initiative (for example, infrastructure, research, strategic, operational support etc.) and to specific individual initiatives reflects the relative importance of the organization's strategic objectives and the anticipated contribution of initiatives to those objectives. As noted in section 3.3, the relationship between portfolio management and strategy is two-way – strategic objectives provide the context within which portfolio management operates; the latter provides a means to engage the change delivery functions in the development and delivery of that strategy and in due course provides evidence on the successful implementation of the strategy.

Aligning change initiatives to strategic objectives can best be achieved via benefits, i.e. by expressing the benefits anticipated from change initiatives in terms consistent with the organization's strategic objectives and targets (for example, improved turnover, customer satisfaction, cost per unit, achievement of desired policy outcomes etc.). This in turn depends on:

Table 4.2 Governance alignment: keys to success

Key	Explanation
Clearly defined roles, responsibilities and accountabilities	The roles of the management board and other key positions with regard to portfolio management should be clearly defined and included in the portfolio management framework – particularly in relation to what decisions are made, where and who is involved.
Portfolio governance is consistent with the wider organizational governance structure	Portfolio governance should reflect the wider organizational governance framework, including for financial, risk and performance management.
Shared understanding	There should be a shared understanding of the portfolio governance framework – and stakeholders should be able to describe how and where portfolio decisions are made.
An agreed escalations process	A PPG/change delivery committee (or equivalent) escalates issues where required to the PDG/investment committee or the management board. There is also an agreed escalation process for sub-portfolios to report exceptions beyond tolerance to the corporate/organization-level portfolio governance bodies.
Aligned meeting schedules	Key meetings of the portfolio boards are scheduled as close together as possible. This facilitates more effective, coordinated decision-making resulting from the consideration of consistent data. A linked issue concerns aligning progress-reporting schedules so that the dashboard represents an up-to-date position.
Sub-portfolios are periodically reviewed by the organizational portfolio governance body	The portfolio governance body should periodically review sub-portfolios to ensure that they are consistent with the organizational portfolio and that initiatives are not being deliberately disaggregated to avoid portfolio governance.

- The existence of a strategy containing well-defined and agreed strategic objectives with associated targets and measures. For example, many organizations have adopted a balanced scorecard with metrics defined for the four perspectives – financial, customer, internal business process, and learning and growth. Where strategic objectives are expressed in clearly measurable terms, this provides a consistent basis for assessing the specific contribution of individual initiatives to the strategic objectives, and this assessment can be used to inform portfolio prioritization (see section 6.4). Assessing strategic contribution is also aided by driver-based analysis as explained below.
- Change initiatives having a reliable business case – not necessarily a long document, but one that demonstrates clearly the business drivers, benefits and the factors affecting their achievability. The benefits should be identified

in sufficient and consistent detail to enable their contribution to the strategic measures to be assessed and compared with other potential investments. Techniques to facilitate this are outlined below.

Figure 4.2 contains a simplified example of how benefits from change initiatives align with strategic objectives. It also identifies a change initiative that is not linked to a strategic objective and which should therefore be reviewed as to whether it should continue or be stopped.

One problem organizations can face is that their strategic objectives are set at such a high level that reliably determining the contribution of individual initiatives, and the portfolio as a whole, is difficult. One solution is to develop a **driver-based model** where the implicit logic or value chain underpinning the strategic objectives is made explicit. For example:

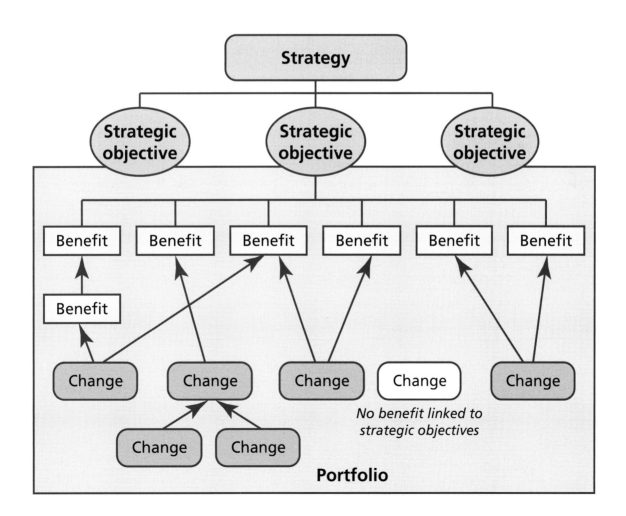

Figure 4.2 Example of alignment of change initiatives with strategic objectives

■ **Private sector** Research at Harvard University[14] has confirmed the link between employee satisfaction and customer satisfaction, and in turn, between customer satisfaction, customer loyalty and the bottom line. This is what the Harvard researchers call the 'service profit chain'. There is consequently a causal chain from employee satisfaction to improved profitability and growth, and this chain is particularly strong between:

- Customer loyalty and company growth and profitability
- Employee and customer satisfaction
- Employee satisfaction and capability.

One company that has used such analyses is Sears, which modelled this relationship mathematically – an 8-unit increase in employee attitude was expected to drive a 1.3-unit increase in customer 'impression' and this in turn drives a 0.5% increase in revenue growth.

■ **Public sector** Ralph Heintzman and Brian Marson[15] have proposed a 'public sector service value chain' from employee engagement (satisfaction and commitment) through client satisfaction to citizen trust and confidence, as illustrated in Figure 4.3.

A similar approach is value profiling as outlined in the *Management of Value* (MoV™) (TSO, 2010) guidance. Here the organization's 'value profile' is established by identifying and prioritizing the organization's 'value drivers', both monetary and non-monetary. Then performance measures for each value driver are determined – against which the benefits realized from change can be mapped to determine the contribution to strategic objectives. This technique can also be used to prioritize initiatives based on performance against the weighted value drivers, or this value score can be divided by the cost to provide a relative value for money index. It is emphasized that such measures are in many cases based on subjective assessments, and consequently the analyses should be used to inform decision-making by senior management rather than being used to make the decision without scope for management discretion. See Figure 4.4 for a simplified example of a value profile.

Such driver-based models[16] can prove valuable in enabling organizations to assess the contribution of initiatives to the drivers that enable and underpin the achievement of the strategic objectives. This is enhanced where strategy modelling and driver analysis is combined with more detailed

Employee satisfaction and commitment		Citizen/client service satisfaction		Citizen trust and confidence in public institutions
↑		↑		↑
Potential drivers		**Drivers**		**Potential drivers**
Career path Fair pay/benefits Value to citizens Work environment Perceptions of management		Timeliness Competence Courtesy Fairness Outcome		Social/cultural factors Macro-performance Micro-performance – Political – Administrative Service satisfaction Service benefit Service adequacy

Figure 4.3 Heintzman and Marson's proposed public sector service value chain

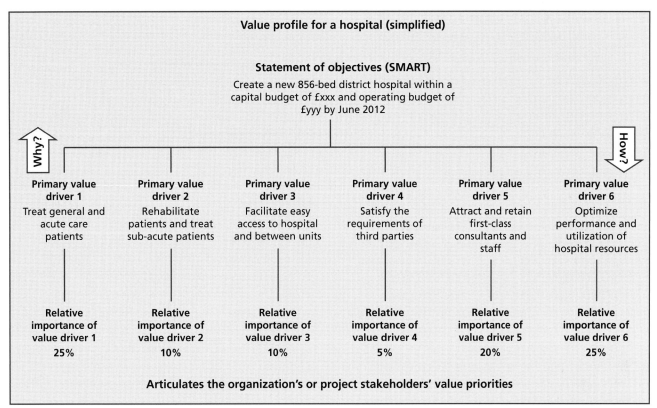

Value profile for a hospital (simplified)

Statement of objectives (SMART)

Create a new 856-bed district hospital within a capital budget of £xxx and operating budget of £yyy by June 2012

Why?

How?

Primary value driver 1	Primary value driver 2	Primary value driver 3	Primary value driver 4	Primary value driver 5	Primary value driver 6
Treat general and acute care patients	Rehabilitate patients and treat sub-acute patients	Facilitate easy access to hospital and between units	Satisfy the requirements of third parties	Attract and retain first-class consultants and staff	Optimize performance and utilization of hospital resources
Relative importance of value driver 1	Relative importance of value driver 2	Relative importance of value driver 3	Relative importance of value driver 4	Relative importance of value driver 5	Relative importance of value driver 6
25%	10%	10%	5%	20%	25%

Articulates the organization's or project stakeholders' value priorities

Figure 4.4 Example of a value profile

initiative-level benefits modelling techniques (for example, benefits dependency networking, strategic contribution analysis, investment logic mapping, and outcome relationship modelling), which demonstrate how benefits will be derived from initiatives and, in turn, how these benefits are related to the strategic drivers. *Managing Successful Programmes* (MSP) (TSO, 2007) and *Management of Value* (MoV) contain more information on the application of benefits modelling and value profiling to programmes and projects.

Important note

Creating benefits models/maps is usually best achieved via the use of workshops with the appropriate mix of operational and change initiative people present. The person leading on the creation of the benefits model/map will require a good understanding of the business context (including the strategic objectives), the required benefits and the potential solutions.

Example: Strategy and benefits mapping

The scope of the UK government's service transformation agreement encompassed six core strategic projects, cross-government initiatives and a range of departmental activity. To facilitate a clear line of sight across this activity, the Cabinet Office developed:

■ A high-level strategy map to show the vision, the strategies by which this vision was to be achieved, and the published measures of strategic success, including improved customer experience, reduced avoidable contact, consolidation of websites and efficiency savings.

■ Benefits logic maps for each core strategic project to show how they would contribute to these measures of strategic success – i.e. a consistent set of maps were completed showing the scope of the change initiatives, the anticipated benefits and how these benefits contributed to the strategic measures of success identified above.

4.5.1 How can the portfolio be aligned with strategy if strategic measures are not clearly defined?

Where measures of strategic success have not been clearly defined, it is still possible to align the portfolio with strategy, although less precisely. Techniques to facilitate this include:

- Portfolio segmentation – i.e. splitting the total available funding into segments to reflect high-level strategic choices on relative importance. Initiatives in each segment are then prioritized on the basis of criteria relevant to that segment. This is discussed further under 'categorize' in section 6.3. This technique has been widely used in the IT portfolio field to make the relative spend on infrastructure transparent and then to manage this down over time to release funds for more business value-adding initiatives.
- Weighting and rating systems – e.g. rating the strategic contribution of an initiative as, for example, mission-critical, highly desirable or desirable. This is discussed further under 'prioritize' in section 6.4.
- Using pair-wise comparisons and decision-conferencing techniques to reach consensus on the relative merits of the various initiatives. A simple spreadsheet can be used to assess initiatives in pairs in terms of their strategic contribution; for example, is initiative A more or less strategically important than initiative B? This approach to assessing strategic alignment is often of most value when it is derived from a facilitated open debate by senior managers. Such decision-conferencing techniques[17] have been found to be very effective – not only in selecting a balanced, strategically aligned portfolio, but also in building commitment to delivery of the portfolio. Under this approach, senior managers consider and debate the weightings to assign to the various strategic objectives, the criteria to be used to assess initiatives and the relevant strategic importance of the various initiatives. In this way they come to a collective decision on the composition of the portfolio.

Example: Ensuring strategy drives portfolio decisions[18]

In HMRC, the first test of any proposed initiative is to ensure that it is aligned with the strategic objectives and priorities. Consequently, each initiative must engage with, and secure sign-off from, the Strategic Design and Gateway Authority (SDA). This ensures that investment initiatives meet HMRC design principles before any recommendations are put to the investment committee. This not only ensures the strategic alignment of potential portfolio initiatives, it also reduces nugatory business case development work for initiatives that are not included in the portfolio and are effectively terminated at the earliest opportunity.

Example: Aligning the portfolio with strategy[19]

East Hampshire District Council chief executive, Will Godfrey, wanted to improve the corporate planning process to ensure the manifesto of any incoming democratically elected council could be adequately reflected in the strategic planning process and priorities set accordingly. He wanted a strategic decision-making process that could support their business and financial planning while fully engaging both elected members and council officers. The process needed to be transparent and provide a clear framework in which councillors could be in control.

Supported by Ferris Cowper, leader of East Hampshire District Council, he introduced corporate portfolio management with decision-conferencing. The process allowed the councillors to prioritize the various growth and savings options brought forward by the different department heads and service groups in an open, transparent, inclusive and objective manner. The final portfolio provided a balance of activities, delivered greater value for money, and aligned with the incoming elected council's vision. Furthermore, the involvement of both the officers and the councillors in prioritizing the portfolio ensured they were aligned and committed to the strategic plan.

The target situation

Our organization has a strategic plan containing well-defined and agreed strategic objectives, each one also having associated targets and measures, which we review regularly and update as required.

In developing the portfolio to deliver the strategic objectives, the portfolio office works closely with the performance and strategic planning teams.

The strategic planning process is on a three-year cycle, incorporating an annual plan that defines the strategy in more detail – this includes information on the performance targets and planned change initiatives for that year. Initially, we thought this could be our portfolio plan but we quickly discovered that we needed a more granular plan with a top-level overview and the facility to drill down to understand the component initiatives. So we now compile a portfolio delivery plan each year along with a summary and links to online portfolio information.

This cycle works well because the PDG/investment committee goes through a portfolio review and prioritization process every six months. This ensures that the portfolio remains aligned with the strategic objectives. (Sometimes strategic objectives need to be amended due to changes in the external environment such as new legislation.) So doing this every six months not only maintains alignment, but also ensures that the portfolio prioritization remains up to date and resources continue to be allocated in the right places. This also maintains focus on collaborative working and ensures that people are engaged continually throughout the life of the portfolio.

Table 4.3 Strategy alignment: keys to success

Key	Explanation
Strategic objectives are supported by driver-based analysis	An organizational strategy exists, containing well-defined and agreed strategic objectives with associated targets and measures. Driver-based models and analysis are used to make the implicit value/logic chain explicit.
Benefits are clearly and consistently identified	The benefits and strategic contribution of each change initiative are defined in a business case on a consistent basis (see coverage of the portfolio benefits framework in section 7.3). This will help the performance contribution to be understood and initiatives to be appraised and prioritized on a level playing field (environment in which all companies compete under the same conditions).
Collaborative working	The portfolio office works closely with strategic planning and performance management departments/functions in linking the forecast impact of the portfolio with the strategic objectives and performance targets – and validating performance claims in business cases.
Regular review at a portfolio level	A full review of the portfolio should take place on a regular basis (six-monthly works well in many organizations depending on the scale of environmental changes and the stability of the strategic objectives) and at least annually, to ensure the portfolio remains aligned with the strategic objectives.
Regular review at an initiative level	Use of a business change lifecycle helps ensure that the strategic alignment of individual initiatives is reviewed at key points in the programme or project lifecycle via regular stage/phase gates.
Early involvement improves quality	Involvement of key departments/functions that will appraise potential investments early in the development of the business case enhances collaborative working and the quality of business cases.

4.6 PORTFOLIO MANAGEMENT PRINCIPLE 4: PORTFOLIO OFFICE

Portfolio management enables the relevant portfolio governance bodies to make better and more informed investment decisions. A function (physical or virtual) is therefore required to provide timely and accurate information to facilitate that decision-making process. The key services provided by this function include:

- Defining portfolio-wide PPM standards, processes and templates to ensure consistent approaches are applied and to provide a clear line of sight across the portfolio.
- Providing an assurance to senior management on effective and efficient management and delivery of change initiatives.
- Providing a challenge or critical-friend role for individual initiatives. (A critical friend is a trusted person who offers critiques of a work as a friend.)
- Providing support, advice and guidance to individual change initiatives – whilst ensuring that this does not compromise the portfolio office's independence from the delivery functions by, for example, ensuring different staff provide the support and assurance/challenge functions.
- Preparing the portfolio strategy and delivery plan (see section 6.6 and Appendix E).
- Coordinating and participating in stage/phase gate, investment appraisal, portfolio-level prioritization and progress reviews.
- Preparing the portfolio dashboard.
- Improving the links and feedback loop between policy and strategy formulation and PPM delivery.

A popular option is the adoption of the P3O model, which is defined as a decision-enabling and support business model for all business change within an organization. This will include single or multiple physical or virtual structures, i.e. offices (permanent and/or temporary) providing a mix of central and localized functions and services, integration with governance arrangements and the wider business such as other corporate support functions.

As the P3O guidance stresses, however, there is no 'one size fits all' approach, and the size and scope of the portfolio office will vary from organization to organization. For example, it could be a physical team (this is usually the case in most large organizations), or it could be a virtual team. The critical points are that to be fully effective the portfolio office should:

- Have sufficient organizational status to help overcome silo-based interests and to demonstrate the importance of effective portfolio management across the organization. Ideally, the portfolio office should report into the top of the organization (for example, to the business change or portfolio director).
- Be sufficiently independent of PPM delivery so that its analyses are objective and credible and it is not accused of being biased.
- Be skilled to ensure that the analyses produced are reliable and timely.

This does not necessarily mean significant additional spend or bureaucracy – indeed experience shows that savings are possible from improved coordination, integration and streamlining of existing functions and processes.

4.6.1 Portfolio, programme and project offices

The P3O guidance provides detailed information on all elements of a portfolio, programme and project office. P3O highlights that a portfolio office provides the means to do the following:

- Establish a structure for selecting the right programmes and projects for the organization.
- Ensure ongoing alignment of programmes and projects with strategic objectives and targets.
- Assess whether new requirements can be accommodated within existing organizational capability, capacity and maturity.
- Allocate the right resources to the right programmes and projects.
- Ensure scrutiny and challenge.
- Identify and manage dependencies between programmes and projects.
- Resolve conflicts for scarce and costly resources (these could be technical, PPM or business resources).
- Assist with identification of threats and opportunities and evaluate the true implications of the aggregate level of programme and project risk.
- Monitor progress of programmes and projects against key objectives.

- Ensure ongoing successful delivery of programmes and projects.
- Adopt value management – active management of the portfolio to optimize value, realize benefits and feed back learning into the investment selection and portfolio prioritization process.
- Achieve value-for-money savings and efficiency gains from programme and project rationalization.
- Ensure the organization has a balanced portfolio, with consideration given to the ability of the organization to absorb change with the least disruption to BAU.
- Link change benefits to the performance management structure.
- Ensure investment in research and development activities for the long-term survival of the organization.

A portfolio office is not simply a bigger programme or project office. In summary, portfolio offices differ from programme and project offices in the following ways:

- Programme and project offices are primarily concerned with coordinating the delivery of individual change initiatives in the right way. Portfolio offices are primarily concerned with ensuring these initiatives remain strategically aligned, coordinating delivery at a collective level (addressing dependencies and portfolio-level risks, and managing constraints to optimize delivery), monitoring benefits realization, ensuring that senior management receive relevant and timely information on the performance of the portfolio, and checking that lessons learned are identified, disseminated and applied.
- Programme and project offices are temporary structures set up to support a specific change initiative. Portfolio offices are usually permanent and integrated into the organizational governance structure. Ideally, they should have direct contact with, and report to, the management board.

Figure 4.5 illustrates the high-level outline P3O model.

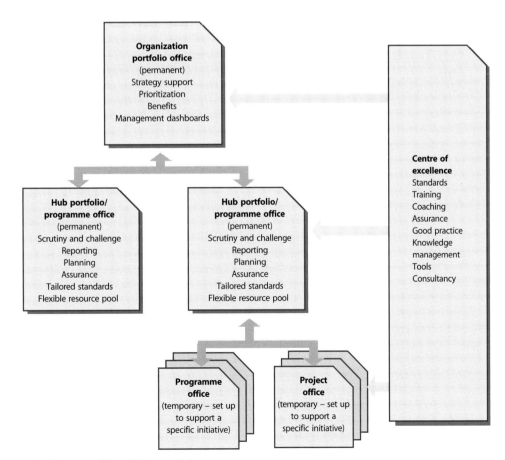

Figure 4.5 Example of an outline P3O model

The target situation

A portfolio office has been established, reporting to the business change director, who is a management board member and portfolio management champion. Initially, when the portfolio office was set up, some people thought it would be a bureaucratic overhead. That was until the portfolio office vision and blueprint[20] was agreed by the management board, which enabled everyone to understand what it would mean for them and how things would work in the future.

Since then the portfolio office has implemented and managed the business change lifecycle and published it on the intranet with all the related documents and guidance. Initially, people didn't want to invest the time to write a business case and a realistic programme/project plan, but once they saw that the management board actually used the information and advice from the portfolio office to agree (and reject) business cases, this changed. Everyone realized that if their initiative was agreed it would be included in the portfolio, which meant the initiative had the board's full commitment and it would be resourced appropriately. Although some were unhappy because their initiative was ultimately given a lower priority (or was even stopped), they recognized that the decision was made in the interests of the organization as a whole – senior management support was crucial in making this happen.

The portfolio office now publishes a portfolio dashboard each month, which reports the progress of the initiatives within the portfolio to the management board. This means that programme managers (and some project managers) have to provide standard progress or highlight reports. Initially, this was an effort, but because people now plan their initiatives more rigorously and the portfolio office uses standard templates and an agreed reporting schedule, it has become far easier; plus managers know that if they raise an issue it will be addressed by those with the authority to make a difference – so it is worth the effort. The portfolio dashboard is also published on our intranet each month so everyone can see how the information provided is used and what progress is being made.

The portfolio office also does other things that are important to the delivery of the portfolio (for example, engaging with other key departments to make sure that people work together and have a common understanding of the portfolio). The portfolio office is experienced in PPM and strategy, so the direct support it provides to the programme and project managers is credible and welcomed, especially with things like business case development, benefits modelling/mapping workshops, dependency workshops and helping to work though the business change lifecycle.

Table 4.4 Portfolio office: keys to success

Key	Explanation
Organizational status	The portfolio office must report directly to the management board champion to help overcome silo-based interests and to demonstrate the importance of effective portfolio management to the organization. It should also be independent of any PPM delivery responsibility to ensure that its analyses are objective.
An agreed mandate	The management board agree the portfolio office terms of reference or vision and blueprint, which will support the implementation of portfolio management across the organization.
Collaborative working	The portfolio office focuses on collaborative working with functions such as BAU; strategic/business planning; budgeting and resource allocation; project and programme management; performance management; corporate governance; and with those in other functions such as commercial, IT and HR with a role in delivery of the organization's strategic objectives.
Appropriate skills	The portfolio office team is appropriately skilled and experienced to ensure that its reports are credible. These skills include strategic planning, investment appraisal, programme and project management, risk management, benefits management and financial management.
Regular measurement of progress	The portfolio office regularly reviews progress and adapts its activities, and the portfolio management processes, accordingly.

4.7 PORTFOLIO MANAGEMENT PRINCIPLE 5: ENERGIZED CHANGE CULTURE

Effective portfolio management is more than a series of principles and practices – success can only truly be realized if the people working for the organization are engaged, focused on the appropriate goals and feel a sense of working together as one team. The portfolio management cycles of definition and delivery (see Figure 0.1) are driven by organizational energy, and in the context of portfolio management an energized change culture includes elements such as:

- Senior management commitment, communication and motivation (see section 4.3).
- A mutual and shared desire to succeed based on effective employee engagement (see section 7.6).
- Effective governance with an appropriate level of bureaucracy (see section 4.4 and section 7.7).
- Culture and behaviours reflective of a focus on the overall good and success of the organization rather than individual or silo-based interests.

See the further consideration of organizational energy in section 5.5.

Important note

An organization will have a finite amount of energy and therefore should regularly assess its capacity to deliver initiatives and to absorb business change, both from the perspective of the programme and project community and from that of the recipients of the change.

The target situation

We were launching the five-year strategy and decided to introduce portfolio management at the same time. We did this for a number of reasons. First, because we knew that the improvements included in the strategy were extremely tough and high-risk and that they would only be realized if everyone pulled in the same direction. Secondly, we were conscious of an internal perception that 'the strategy is just a document that gets produced and does not really affect me.' Finally, we felt that while a clear strategy is critical in terms of talking about where you are going and how you are going to get there, we needed a vehicle to actually get us there. Portfolio management was seen as that vehicle.

This presented us with a challenge: we needed to make the whole organization feel engaged, inspired and motivated to face the challenge ahead positively.

Historically, the organizational strategy was created by the management board alone. However, this time a series of consultation workshops were used which enabled people to be engaged and to present questions directly to the management board.

The management board's communication of the strategy and the portfolio was designed to be much more engaging, informative and compelling, and it translated the strategy into real-life situations in a way that people could instantly relate to. A key message was that people working in the organization were viewed as part of one team and not just individual departments – everyone was important in developing the new strategy and everyone had a role to play in its success. A vital part of this was to review people's objectives (starting with the management board) and make sure they were aligned to the strategic objectives. In some cases the actual success of the portfolio was linked to people's objectives and bonuses.

An HR project was also included in the portfolio, which focused on people's well-being. We asked people what they wanted and, most importantly, we listened and implemented the ideas where we could. This included better facilities such as a crèche and gym, flexible working time, more relaxing office interiors, home-working, investment in training and a range of other things. Whilst only a small number of the ideas were implemented initially, they seemed to have an almost instantaneous positive effect.

Communication became a critical aspect when the change initiatives started to deliver successfully, because historically people did not have the time or the energy to celebrate success. This is not the case now, and we make sure that everyone knows when there has been a success. When things are tough, people work together to turn things around.

Table 4.5 Energized change culture: keys to success

Key	Explanation
Collaborative working	View the organization as one team and focus on creating a collaborative environment including adapting the performance management and reward and recognition systems to reflect and encourage the desired behaviours.
Proactive communications	Ensure that regular, proactive and compelling communication is published about the objectives of the portfolio and progress made.
A learning organization	Create an environment in which lessons learned are captured, disseminated and acted upon – using post-implementation reviews, online learning centres and lessons-learned workshops.
Clarity about expectations	Train people in the business change lifecycle so that they understand what is expected of them.
Effective processes	Portfolio management processes must add value and be perceived as consistent, transparent, accurate, objective and fair. In addition, align these processes with those related to strategic planning and financial management. Use the champion–challenger model and encourage all stakeholders to suggest enhancements.
Roles and relationships agreed with a clear line of sight from strategic to personal objectives	Document roles and relationships. Ensure that the role descriptions focus on performance and help people to understand their contribution to the strategic objectives.
Monitoring of organizational energy	Undertake surveys to assess the types and depth of energy that exist within the organization and/or in individual teams.
Demonstrable senior management commitment	Senior management should actually do what they say in personally and consistently demonstrating commitment to the new ways of working.
Listening and engagement	Involve people, listen to them and encourage them to contribute. Ensure that they can see how their contribution has been incorporated into the portfolio. Include feedback from key stakeholders in the portfolio performance metrics (see Appendix F).

Portfolio management cycles

5

5 Portfolio management cycles

5.1 PURPOSE OF THIS CHAPTER

This chapter re-introduces the two portfolio management cycles and considers the main approaches to implementing portfolio management and how to sustain progress, including the role of organizational energy in ensuring success. The discussion then lays the foundation for more detailed consideration of the portfolio management practices in Chapters 6 and 7 by examining the purpose of the definition and delivery cycles, what happens when they are managed effectively and what happens when this is not the case.

5.2 THE PORTFOLIO MANAGEMENT CYCLES

The portfolio management cycles were introduced in Chapter 2 and are illustrated in Figure 0.1.

Portfolio management does not have a mandated start point, middle or end – rather:

- The definition cycle contains a series of broadly sequential practices (i.e. 'understand' generally comes before 'categorize', which usually comes before 'prioritize' etc.), although in practice they will often overlap.

- The delivery cycle is different in that the practices here are undertaken broadly simultaneously; but the cycle analogy is still applicable as the individual initiatives go through the programme or project lifecycle, and as portfolio delivery is linked to the strategic planning, financial and risk management cycles.

5.3 IF THERE IS NO DEFINED START, HOW SHOULD PORTFOLIO MANAGEMENT BE IMPLEMENTED?

Different organizations have different reasons for implementing portfolio management, including: a major cut in budgets forcing questions about how to achieve deficit reduction without impacting adversely on service delivery; an external event such as a new competitor or regulatory change;

a new chief executive officer; or the realization that the organization's track record in delivery of change initiatives and benefits realization requires corrective action. Similarly, organizations have different starting points reflecting their existing PPM capability, organizational culture, governance structure, financial position and strategic objectives. The different drivers behind the adoption of portfolio management, and the differing conditions in which it is undertaken, will influence the way in which portfolio management is implemented. Three broad approaches can be identified as outlined in Table 5.1.

It is important to emphasize that there is no one right way to implement portfolio management – it all depends on the circumstances.

Table 5.1 Approaches to implementing portfolio management

Big bang	Implementing portfolio management is viewed as a business change programme in its own right and is planned with: ▪ A business case ▪ A compelling vision for the future state ▪ A blueprint or target operating model ▪ An implementation plan agreed by the management board. Here a time-bound implementation phase is followed by live running encompassing all portfolio definition and delivery practices.
Evolution	Here a more evolutionary or incremental approach is taken, starting with areas of greatest need or those where rapid progress can be made. The organization's approach to portfolio management then evolves to reflect its needs, opportunities and lessons learned.
Ad hoc	As with the evolutionary approach, there is no detailed master plan, but there is no expectation that the approach will develop and no commitment to capturing lessons learned to inform development. Instead, implementation is more opportunistic.

The 'big bang' approach is most appropriate where top-down approaches to strategy formulation are applied, where the environment is relatively stable and where PPM is already relatively mature.

In other situations, a staged, incremental or evolutionary approach will be more appropriate – building on initial developments in one part of the organization and focusing on specific processes to demonstrate the value of a portfolio management approach. Indeed, the P3O guidance recommends that an incremental approach be taken to reduce the potential adverse impacts of a big bang implementation.

Guidance on where to start with portfolio management was included in Chapter 2. As the value is proved and support grows, so a more comprehensive, end-to-end approach can be developed. This approach can be very effective – for example, one organization that has been the subject of several case studies on its approach to portfolio management is Hewlett-Packard, where the development was 'evolutionary not revolutionary'.[21] Such evolutionary approaches are particularly relevant in less stable environments and where strategy is itself emergent (i.e. in complex environments where strategy evolves as the organization learns more about 'what works'). In such circumstances the portfolio management approach needs to reflect this in a flexible approach to implementation. However, even where this is the case, it is important to implement portfolio management as a business change programme where the desired end state is kept in mind and regular reviews are undertaken to assess progress and determine the next steps.

In other circumstances a more ad hoc approach will be adopted – this can be the case where existing practices are less mature and where senior commitment to organization-wide, end-to-end portfolio management is less well embedded. In such circumstances, a less structured approach may be the only one feasible, although it should be recognized that planned approaches, whether big bang or evolutionary, do have several advantages:

- Planned approaches to the implementation of business change are supported by Best Management Practice guidance.
- Experience shows that the use of structured, systematic processes drastically improves the likelihood of success.

- A planned approach, with confirmed senior management buy-in, will significantly reduce the risk of failure. Ideally, a board-level member should fill the role of SRO for the implementation of portfolio management.
- Planned approaches can be quicker, so the potential benefits are realized earlier.

5.4 HOW IS PROGRESS SUSTAINED?

After an encouraging start, many implementations of portfolio management rapidly run into difficulties. Notwithstanding investments in staff, training and new software, the whole process can become bogged down in internal politics, silo-based interests and inertia. The lessons learned from those who have avoided or overcome these issues are that continued progress is assisted by incorporating the following factors:

- A senior-level sponsor to maintain focus at the highest level and to continually promote a portfolio-level view.
- An incremental or staged approach, starting with areas of greatest need to demonstrate the value of portfolio management with some 'quick wins'.
- Building on existing organizational processes and not reinventing wheels or changing things that do not need changing.
- Being clear about the success criteria.
- Regular assessment of progress – not just in terms of meeting milestones, but more significantly in relation to the benefits realized and progress against the agreed success criteria. See Appendix F.
- Effective and ongoing stakeholder engagement and communications.
- Aligning the reward and recognition processes with the appropriate behaviours (i.e. taking a corporate rather than departmental or functional perspective) – and enforcing them through objective-setting and personal reviews. This is especially important for senior management, programme managers and budget holders.
- Adopting a champion–challenger model where processes are open to challenge and improvement – but until successfully challenged, all agree to adhere to the current process. This helps to ensure that stakeholders are actively involved in the portfolio practices

rather than perceiving them as something that is done to them.

- A commitment to continuous improvement, including identifying improvements to the portfolio management practices via membership of appropriate professional groups, capturing lessons learned from robust post-implementation reviews, submissions under the champion–challenger model and periodic portfolio effectiveness reviews (including those using a relevant maturity framework such as P3M3).
- Appropriate use of software tools tailored to support organizational needs. It was noted in Chapter 2 that software solutions are not a prerequisite for effective portfolio management although, that said, the appropriate use of tools which are tailored to the organizational requirements can help embed the new ways of working as BAU.

Sustaining progress is also dependent on the commitment of key stakeholders (most crucially, senior management) and the existence of sufficient organizational energy.

5.5 WHY DOES ORGANIZATIONAL ENERGY LINK THE PORTFOLIO MANAGEMENT CYCLES?

The concept of organizational energy, which was introduced in the last chapter, is a significant consideration in many organizations, particularly those that recognize that human capital is the most precious of all assets and those where the scale of change is increasing. The NHS Institute for Innovation and Improvement[22] has defined organizational energy as 'the extent to which an organization has mobilized the full available effort of its people in pursuit of its goals'. This definition is based on research in the Organizational Energy Programme at the University of St Gallen, Switzerland, and by Henley Business School, who similarly define organizational energy as 'the extent to which an organization (or division or team) has mobilized its emotional, cognitive and behavioural potential to pursue its goals.'[23]

Bruch and Vogel[24] identify four energy states:

- **Productive energy** People with high emotional involvement are on the lookout for new opportunities and take decisive action to solve problems because they really care about the success of the organization.

- **Comfortable energy** There is a relaxed atmosphere and people prefer the status quo.
- **Resigned energy** People are mentally withdrawn and do nothing more than is required of them.
- **Corrosive energy** People experience high levels of anger, fight each other, and actively hinder change and innovation.

When these types of energy are mapped on a matrix using the axes of 'intensity' and 'quality' as in Figure 5.1, a picture can emerge that will enable organizations to plan a route from where they are to where they want to be – with the ideal being within the 'productive energy' quadrant. Movement to this quadrant requires the development of a shared vision to which the portfolio contributes, clear leadership and a range of initiatives that engage staff and ignite the sources of organizational energy. These sources of energy have been identified as:[25]

- **Connection** – how people link themselves, their values and their work to the purpose of the organization.
- **Content** – work stimulates and provides a sense of achievement.
- **Context** – working practices support and enable people to do a good job.
- **Climate** – how the organization helps people to grow, achieve their potential and do their best.

It is critical to appreciate that whilst portfolio management will enable informed decision-making, without the collective, coordinated effort of all those involved (and management of that effort) the delivery of the portfolio and contribution to strategic objectives will be at risk. Staff engagement is considered in section 7.6.

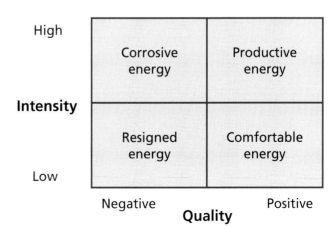

Figure 5.1 Organizational energy matrix

5.6 PORTFOLIO DEFINITION CYCLE

5.6.1 What is the purpose?

The purpose of the portfolio definition cycle is to collate key information that will provide clarity to senior management on the collection of change initiatives which will deliver the greatest contribution to the strategic objectives, subject to consideration of risk/achievability, resource constraints and cost/affordability. The key output of the portfolio definition cycle is an understanding of what the portfolio is going to deliver – encapsulated in a portfolio strategy (the long-term view of the portfolio and its contribution to strategic objectives) and a portfolio delivery plan which focuses on the forthcoming planning period. Together, these documents will reflect the decisions taken by the management board (or sub-boards when portfolio functions are delegated) regarding the scope, contents, key milestones, costs, risks and the results anticipated from delivering the portfolio successfully.

5.6.2 What happens if this is done well?

The overriding benefit of the portfolio definition cycle is its focus on providing clarity on the high-level scope, schedule, dependencies, risks, costs (and affordability) and benefits of the potential change initiatives – which in turn enables the portfolio governance body to make informed decisions on the composition of the portfolio to optimize strategic contribution.

Defining the portfolio does not mean that everything in the portfolio must be planned in detail. Indeed, it would be wrong to attempt to do this because that is the role of programme and project management. However, a clear line of sight on the high-level milestones, estimated cost and resource requirements, risks, dependencies and benefits provides a basis for a shared understanding of the portfolio and managing progress. It also ensures that the organization matches the planned changes with its capacity to deliver without over-committing or, alternatively, having excess idle resources.

5.6.3 What if this is not done well?

If the portfolio definition cycle is not managed well, there is a high risk that the portfolio will not represent the best use of available resources in the context of the organization's strategic objectives and aggregate risk; pet projects will consume resources at the expense of higher-priority initiatives; activities will be started without considering their fit with the current portfolio; and delivery will be impacted with too many or poorly scheduled initiatives with conflicting resource requirements and unbalanced impacts on BAU.

5.7 PORTFOLIO DELIVERY CYCLE

5.7.1 What is the purpose?

The purpose of the portfolio delivery cycle is to ensure the successful implementation of the planned change initiatives as agreed in the portfolio strategy and delivery plan, whilst also ensuring that the portfolio adapts to changes in the strategic objectives, project and programme delivery and lessons learned.

5.7.2 What happens if this is done well?

Resources, risks and dependencies will be efficiently and effectively managed, and senior management will gain greater control over the change portfolio. This in turn will enable improved delivery on time and to budget, whilst facilitating benefits realization and helping to ensure that the portfolio remains strategically aligned by enabling resource reallocation when required.

5.7.3 What if this is not done well?

Portfolio delivery is aligned to the organizational strategy, which means it will be managed over a number of years (usually three or four years, although some large organizations plan strategically for five or ten years). During that time, organizational and environmental change will occur. If the portfolio delivery cycle is not managed effectively in the context of these changes, many initiatives will not be delivered on time and to budget; demand and supply for resources will not be matched, resulting in shortages and idle capacity; inadequate action will be taken to address poor performance and slippage; initiative scheduling will result in unnecessary operational disruption; the portfolio will not adjust to shifts in business priorities and consequently money will be spent unwisely; and the contribution to strategic objectives will not be optimized.

Portfolio definition cycle: practices 1–5

6 Portfolio definition cycle: practices 1–5

6.1 PURPOSE OF THIS CHAPTER

This chapter provides a more detailed discussion of the five practices found within the portfolio definition cycle:

- Understand
- Categorize
- Prioritize
- Balance
- Plan.

For ease of reading, each practice is described by answering the following two questions:

- What is the purpose?
- What is involved?

Real-life examples are included to illustrate the application of these practices – although it should be recognized that they should be adapted to suit the specific organizational circumstances. Keys to success for each of the five practices are given in Tables 6.1, 6.3 and 6.7–6.9, respectively.

6.2 PORTFOLIO MANAGEMENT PRACTICE 1: UNDERSTAND

6.2.1 What is the purpose?

During the strategic planning process, strategic objectives will be developed and the changes need to achieve those strategic objectives will be identified. During this process the management board will need to also consider the existing change initiatives and those in the project development pipeline, together with their forecast impact on organizational performance. The collection of such information is usually coordinated by the portfolio office utilizing some form of programme and project information document (see Appendix C). This is the top-down or strategic approach to portfolio management, where the portfolio is designed to deliver the changes required to achieve the defined strategic objectives. There is another approach that is more appropriate in more dynamic environments and where strategy is emergent – here change initiatives are proposed bottom-up and are appraised and prioritized on a regular basis in the context of the current high-level strategic objectives, which themselves adapt as a result of new understanding about what works and shifts in the environment in which the organization operates.

Whichever approach is adopted, top-down or bottom-up (or a combination), the purpose of the 'understand' practice is the same – to obtain a clear and transparent view of what is in the current portfolio and the project development pipeline, performance to date and, looking forward, the forecast costs, benefits, and risks to delivery and benefits realization.

6.2.2 What is involved?

During strategic planning the portfolio office will work closely with the strategy team. For example, the portfolio office will provide information relating to a review of the existing portfolio. If a portfolio does not yet formally exist, the portfolio office will undertake a review of existing change initiatives to assess information such as planned business impact, forecast benefits, costs and resources required, risk and performance to date. Undertaking such a review where a portfolio does not yet formally exist is important because in most cases portfolio management will not be introduced to a 'greenfield' or undeveloped site; i.e. there will be a range of current initiatives in planning, under development and in delivery. Identifying these initiatives (both those that are 'live' and those that are at the concept stage) can be far from straightforward, and it helps if the portfolio office starts with some idea of what sort of initiatives are potentially to be included in the portfolio – for example, those above a minimum financial cost (note the discussion at 4.4.2.3). Even more fundamentally, what constitutes a 'project' or 'programme' can be a consideration. This task is also aided by working through a standard template (such as the programme and project information template shown in Appendix C), which will help to capture consistent information for each initiative.

In determining the strategic objectives, the management board will consider information about the current portfolio, along with that from other areas of the organization (including BAU, current and planned performance information, budgetary allocations etc.) and environmental analyses using approaches such as:

- **SWOT analysis** – strengths, weaknesses, opportunities and threats.
- **PESTLE analysis** – considering factors such as political, economic, social, technological, legal and environmental.
- **Porter's five forces analysis** – rivalry, threat of substitutes, buyer power, supplier power and barriers to entry.

Once the strategic objectives are determined, the next step is to perform a gap analysis – to determine the gap between where the organization will be on the current trajectory incorporating planned changes and where it needs to be if it is to achieve the strategic objectives. The next step will be to identify the change initiatives required to close this gap. It is essential that the portfolio office is engaged in this debate because not only can it provide a framework for identifying and appraising potential initiatives, but during

the discussions it can also advise on the impact on the current portfolio and resource considerations, which are often forgotten in the freedom of blue-sky thinking.

The output of the 'understand' practice will be a clear view of the portfolio and its constituent programmes and projects – both those that are live and those that are in the planning phase. Many organizations have found that just completing this picture adds significant value by identifying duplicate, low-priority and poorly performing change initiatives that are consuming resources to the detriment of other, more strategically aligned initiatives. This then enables resources to be reallocated to deliver more, and often from less.

Example: Understand the current portfolio

A portfolio analysis of a large oil and gas company found that only one major field was being funded at an optimal level; some warranted greater resources whereas other development plans were over-resourced. The resulting resource reallocation added approximately $1 billion to shareholder value or about 10% of total business value.[26]

Table 6.1 Understand: keys to success

Key	Explanation
A clear portfolio scope	Collecting consistent data on the scope of the current portfolio is greatly aided where clear guidance exists about what constitutes a project or programme and what type of initiatives are to be included in the portfolio.
Consistent data	A standard programme and project information template can help ensure a consistent set of data is collected on all initiatives – and this aids categorization and prioritization in due course.
Sufficient research	Time spent understanding the initiatives and populating the programme and project information template pays dividends during the remainder of the portfolio definition cycle.
Collaborative working between the portfolio office and strategic planning function	The portfolio office works closely with the strategic planning function to ensure that all initiatives relevant to the strategic objectives are identified, including those at the concept stage.
Effective relationships with PPM professionals	Populating the programme and project information template should be used as an opportunity not only to validate the data collected but also to build effective working relationships with PPM professionals.
Preparation of an interim status report	Collate the programme and project information templates into an interim report for the management board, providing a clear view on the contents of the portfolio, any apparent overlaps and duplication, and the associated costs, dependencies, resource requirements, forecast benefits and strategic contribution.

6.3 PORTFOLIO MANAGEMENT PRACTICE 2: CATEGORIZE

6.3.1 What is the purpose?

Categorization organizes change initiatives into groups, segments or sub-portfolios based on the strategic objectives or other groupings as required. The investment criteria used to appraise and prioritize initiatives can then be tailored to suit the specific category or segment. The purpose of the 'categorize' practice is to make it easier for senior decision makers to understand the make-up of their portfolio and thus to make decisions on balance and on the optimum use of available funding and other resources. It can also aid strategic alignment, as the allocation of available resources to individual segments should reflect their relative priorities. Categorization also enables more effective management of portfolio delivery, as a clear view is provided on the different types of changes (legacy/mandatory/transformational/innovative etc.) without them getting lost in the detail of a large general portfolio.

6.3.2 What is involved?

Organizations will categorize their initiatives in different ways, including by strategic objective; line of business; geographical area; type of initiative undertaken (for example, infrastructure and applications, or cost savings and revenue generation) etc. Figure 6.1 illustrates the approach developed by Cranfield University[27] for the Information Systems investment portfolio – although it can be, and has been, applied successfully to business changes more generally.

The number of categories is not limited to four – indeed, the portfolio management guidance issued by the OGC in 2004 referred to the following seven categories: mandatory, strategic, business support, experimental, infrastructure, maintenance and cross-organizational. For the purposes of this guide, the focus will be on the use of categories that are based on the organization's strategic objectives. Where this is the case, initiatives can be categorized by relating their benefits to the appropriate strategic objectives – approaches to achieving this (including via driver-based analysis) were discussed in section 4.5. In some cases, the organization may establish 'entry criteria' for a given category – i.e. only initiatives that contribute a minimum amount of value to the strategic objective will be assessed for inclusion in the relevant portfolio segment or category.

Sometimes it may be appropriate to break down each category into sub-categories – for example, 'Reducing crime' may be too broad a category and so it would be useful to have a number of sub-categories indicating the type of crime and/or geographical area. This in turn helps to assess the strategic contribution of each initiative as the strategic objectives are expressed in more granular/detailed form.

Strategic Investments in IS/IT applications which are *critical* to sustaining future business strategy	**High potential** Investments in IS/IT applications which may be important in achieving future success
Key operational Investments in IS/IT applications on which the organization currently depends for success	**Support** Investments in IS/IT applications which are valuable but not critical to success

Figure 6.1 Cranfield Information Systems investment portfolio

Table 6.2 Simplified portfolio categorization model

Strategic objectives	Category	Change 1	Change 2	Change 3	Change 4	Change 5	Change 6	Change 7	Change 8	Change 9
Improve response times	Call handling	✓			✓					
	Radio		✓							
Improve public access to services	Interactive website			✓		✓		✓		
	Information					✓			✓	✓
	Partnership working									

The information captured in the programme and project information template can be used to identify in which category (or sub-category) the proposed initiative should be included.

Once each initiative has been allocated to a category, it is useful to review the balance of the portfolio across the categories, and graphical formats can help communicate complex information effectively. Table 6.2 and Figure 6.2 provide simplified examples which highlight the strategic objectives, the portfolio categories and how the proposed change initiatives are aligned. From this it is possible to see that proposed change initiative number 6 is not aligned to any

strategic objective and should be investigated further to ascertain whether it is enabling another key programme or project, or whether it should be stopped. It is also clear that the 'partnership working' category/segment has no initiative contributing to it, and should therefore either be removed as a category or initiatives added if appropriate.

It should be noted that number of changes per category is just one (and an admittedly simplified) example of the way data can be presented. Spend by category, and assessment of the risk:return profile by category are also commonly used (see section 6.5.3).

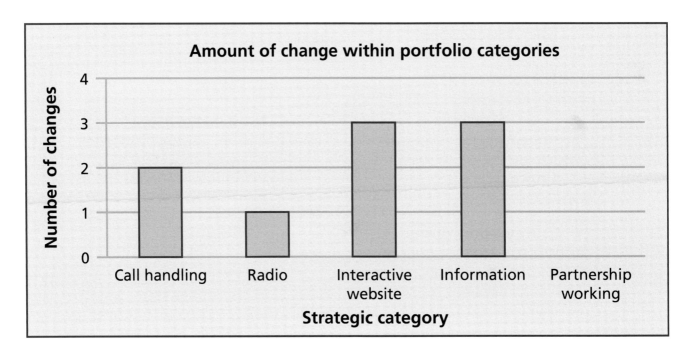

Figure 6.2 Number of changes by portfolio category

Business applications	Mandated
Business applications Justified on non cost-benefit terms – i.e. does the economic value of the benefits exceed the costs?	**Mandated** Justified on cost-benefit terms – any shortfall in benefits represents the implied 'political value' of avoiding non-compliance with the law, regulation or policy.
Replacement infrastructure Justified on cost-benefit terms – i.e. does the replacement enable resources to be re-directed to other value-adding activities?	**New infrastructure** Justified on cost-benefit terms by taking into consideration both the infrastructure and the applications (both planned and potential) that will run on that infrastructure.

Figure 6.3 Example of portfolio categorization with tailored investment criteria

Table 6.3 Categorize: keys to success

Key	Explanation
Use categorization to assess strategic alignment	Data on spend by category provides a high-level check to ensure that resource allocation reflects the relative organizational priorities.
Categories should suit the circumstances	The choice of categorization will vary from organization to organization reflecting the strategic objectives, line of business, geographical area, types of initiative undertaken etc. Where strategic objectives are relatively independent, separate categories can be established as this provides a more granular basis for assessing strategic contribution.
Be creative in presentational formats	The use of creative graphical presentation helps to provide insight into the scope, balance and strategic contribution of the current portfolio.
Tailor the investment criteria	Investment criteria that are used to prioritize initiatives should be tailored to suit each portfolio category or segment. For example, financial metrics are often used for revenue generation and cost-saving categories. In contrast, service/product enhancement categories may use criteria based on scale of enhancement per £/$/€ m invested.
Be sensitive to how the analyses may be perceived	Ensure that relevant stakeholders, including PPM colleagues, are kept up to date with the work being carried out. Be aware that where the analysis indicates that some existing initiatives are not aligned to the strategic objectives (or the contribution is uncertain) this may be perceived as unwelcome news. On the other hand, there should be no 'nasty surprises' when the results are reported to the portfolio governance body.

It is worth highlighting that the relationship of initiatives to category may not always be one to one, and in such cases care needs to be taken that the links from the initiatives to the strategic objectives are well defined. The approaches to strategic alignment and driver-based analysis discussed in section 4.5 are relevant here. Two illustrations of categorization are described in the following examples.

Example: Categorization and tailored investment criteria

This example comes from the UK Criminal Justice System Information Technology (CJS IT) portfolio where available spend was split into portfolio categories or segments and the investment criteria were then tailored in each case as shown in Figure 6.3.

Example: Portfolio segmentation in the European Parliament IT portfolio[28]

The European Parliament IT Directorate has adopted the Val IT™ framework published by the IT Governance Institute. The approach adopted breaks down the portfolio into four different business domains, following the natural division of activities of the parliament, i.e.:

■ Legislative
■ Administrative
■ Communication
■ Members and political groups.

Requests are further broken down along the following axes:

■ How discretionary the spending is, ranging from lowest (e.g. parliament is under a legal obligation to act on the request) to highest (e.g. discretionary spending on new activities).
■ Two investment types (new investment requests as opposed to business-as-usual requests).

6.4 PORTFOLIO MANAGEMENT PRACTICE 3: PRIORITIZE

6.4.1 What is the purpose?

Prioritizing ranks the change initiatives within the portfolio (or portfolio segment) based on one or more agreed measures. The most common measures are financial metrics and/or some form of multi-criteria analysis (MCA) (see section 6.4.2 below). As has already been noted in section 6.3, where segmentation is used the criteria for prioritizing initiatives can be tailored to suit the particular portfolio segments.

The purpose of the 'prioritize' practice is to help senior management and the portfolio governance body answer the following questions – subject to consideration of an appropriate balance between risk and return:

■ Which initiatives should the organization invest in?
■ What are the most important initiatives?
■ What initiatives must be resourced above all others?

6.4.2 What is involved?

The above questions can only be answered when the proposed initiatives have been prioritized, meaning each of the initiatives has been 'ranked' either for the portfolio as a whole or for each segment.

Many organizations employ financial metrics to prioritize initiatives such as 'net present value' (NPV), 'internal rate of return' (IRR) or 'payback'.

■ **NPV** – within the UK central government, the HM Treasury (HMT) *Green Book*[29] recommends that the preferred method of investment appraisal is NPV. Under this approach all future costs and benefits ('sunk' or past costs and benefits are ignored as they are not relevant to today's investment decision) are expressed in monetary value terms, and these values are discounted to today's value using the organization's cost of capital or other discount rate (currently 3.5% in the case of the UK central government). The result is the NPV – a statement of the value of future costs and benefits, expressed at today's value. It is a *monetary* measure.
■ **IRR** – related to NPV as it is the discount rate that expresses future costs and benefits at a zero NPV – in short, the annual percentage return that it is forecast the initiative will achieve. It is a *percentage* measure.
■ **Payback** – how long it takes for the benefits to outweigh the accumulated costs (either discounted or undiscounted). A *time* measure.

Take, for example, an initiative that has a cost/benefit profile over a five-year timeframe as set out in Table 6.4.

Table 6.4 Calculating financial metrics

	Year 0	Year 1	Year 2	Year 3	Year 4	Year 5
Costs (£ m)	50	5	5	5	5	5
Benefits (£ m)	0	15	25	25	20	15
Net flow	−50	10	20	20	15	10
Discount factor	1	0.9662	0.9335	0.9019	0.8714	0.842
Annual NPV	−50.0	9.7	18.7	18.0	13.1	8.4
Cumulative NPV	−50.0	−40.3	−21.7	−3.6	9.4	17.9
IRR						15%

Notes

1 The above analysis follows the convention that year 0 represents initial cash flows and all future cash flows are assumed to occur on the last day of the year for ease of calculation purposes.

2 Net flow represents the excess of benefits over costs.

3 Discount factors are obtained from the HMT *Green Book* for a 3.5% discount rate.

4 Annual NPV represents the net present value of that year's cash flows (benefits less costs).

5 Discounted payback occurs when the cumulative NPV reaches zero and turns positive.

The analysis shows that over a five-year life, the initiative has a net present value of £17.9 m, an internal rate of return of 15% and pays back (in current value terms) in year 4.

Whilst financial metrics are widely used, they do have a number of drawbacks – for example, they can be of limited use where the immediate benefits of the initiative are not financial in nature (the value of a life saved, more engaged staff or infrastructure investments); they can constrain investment in enabling or infrastructure initiatives because the financial return is not immediately obvious; and they assume accurate forecasting of costs and benefits. In relation to the latter point, empirical research shows that forecasts of cost, benefit and duration are often very inaccurate[30] and this clearly compromises effective investment appraisal and portfolio prioritization. One solution is to adjust forecasts for such optimism bias or to use reference class forecasting (see section 7.2.2.2).

Another solution adopted by many organizations is to combine financial metrics with some form of multi-criteria analysis (MCA)[31] considering factors (which may be weighted) under two main headings:

■ The 'return or attractiveness' of each initiative, including such factors as financial return on investment, 'political' need, strategic impact etc. This can be assessed, for example, using the original OGC classifications of mission-critical, highly desirable or desirable[32], or via some measure of strategic contribution (see the discussion of benefits mapping and driver-based analysis in Chapter 4).

■ The 'risk or achievability' of each initiative including such factors as reputational risk, likelihood of project delivery, likelihood of benefits realization, complexity etc. One approach is to base the assessment on the risk potential assessment (RPA)[33] where ratings of risk (very high, high, medium, low and very low) are determined by assessments of 'consequential impact' and 'complexity' (the latter reflecting the four factors of profile, delivery challenge, capacity and capability, and scale). An alternative is to use the delivery confidence assessment now included in the OGC Gateway process, as shown in Figure 6.4, or the approach outlined in the example that follows.

Colour	Criteria description
Green	Successful delivery of the project/programme and its outcomes/benefits to time, cost and quality appears highly likely and there are no major outstanding issues that at this stage appear to threaten delivery significantly.
Amber/Green	Successful delivery appears probable; however, constant attention will be needed to ensure risks do not materialize into major issues threatening delivery.
Amber	Successful delivery appears feasible but significant issues already exist, requiring management attention. These appear resolvable at this stage and, if addressed promptly, should not present a cost/schedule overrun.
Amber/Red	Successful delivery of the project/programme is in doubt with major risks or issues apparent in a number of key areas. Urgent action is needed to ensure that these are addressed, and to decide whether resolution is feasible.
Red	Successful delivery of the project/programme appears to be unachievable. There are major issues on project/programme definition, schedule, budget, required quality or benefits delivery, which at this stage do not appear to be manageable or resolvable. The project/programme may need re-baselining and/or overall viability re-assessed.

Figure 6.4 Delivery confidence

Example: Assessing the likelihood of change initiative success and failure

Research into hundreds of major change programmes across the globe by the Boston Consulting Group (BCG) identified that success is dependent on four elements:

- **Duration** – the time until the project is completed if it has a short life span, or if not, to the next review.

- **Integrity** – the performance integrity or capabilities of the team to deliver the initiative on time including capable and respected leadership, clear objectives, and resources and organizational skills appropriate to the initiative's requirements.

- **Commitment** – to change, including the visible commitment of senior management (C1) and the attitudes of the local area undergoing the change (C2).

- **Effort** – the additional effort over existing responsibilities required of local staff to complete the change.

Assessments ranging from 1 to 4 (where 1 represents the ideal situation) under these headings are made by senior management – a key part of the process is that any differences in perception are openly debated, and although the assessments are subjective, the system provides organizations with a structured basis for discussion and an objective framework for making these assessments.

The resulting ratings are combined in a DICE® score that can be calculated manually (using the formula D+(2I)+(2C1)+C2+E) or by using the calculator at http://dice.bcg.com. The results range from 7 to 28 (the integrity and senior management commitment ratings are assigned a weighting of 2) with the following bandings:

- 7–14 'win' – the initiative is likely to succeed.

- 15–17 'worry' – the initiative's outcome is hard to predict.

- 18–28 'woe' – the initiative is extremely risky and failure is likely.

The results from 225 change initiatives were evaluated using the model, and the results were found to validate the original analysis. Just because an initiative is in the 'woe' category doesn't mean that it should be stopped – rather the focus is on what actions are required to improve the score – and this should be monitored closely to ensure that the scores improve. Similarly, organizations should track the outcomes of projects and compare them with the DICE scores to provide some assurance that scoring is realistic and consistent.

The advantages of the approach, in addition to its simplicity, are that organizations are able to identify problem initiatives in their portfolios on a consistent basis; the open dialogue helps to develop a shared understanding among senior executives; it focuses PPM expertise and senior management attention where it is most needed; and it helps to defuse political issues.

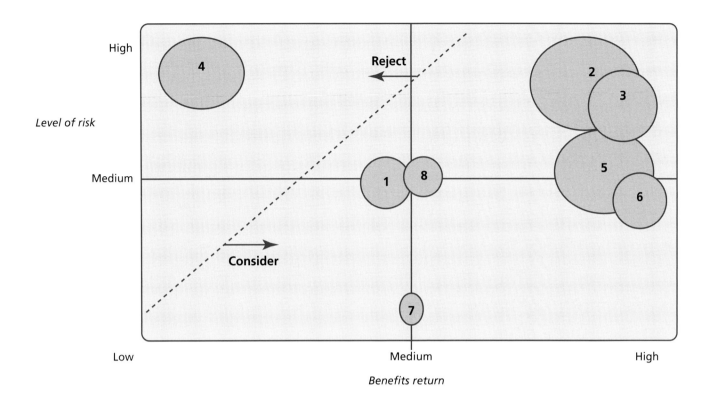

Figure 6.5 Example of a portfolio map 'bubble' matrix of change initiatives based on benefits and risk

Consideration of such factors under the dual headings of 'attractiveness/return' and 'achievability/risk' allows the potential initiatives to be represented in a portfolio map such as is shown in Figure 6.5.

Note: a key decision will be whether to allocate funding to mandatory projects – for example, those in relation to a legal or regulatory requirement – before prioritizing the remaining spend. Alternatively, all initiatives, including mandatory ones, can be included in the prioritization exercise. Some organizations adopt the latter route as it focuses attention on the scale of mandatory spend and ensures that the options selected to meet a mandatory requirement are cost-efficient when viewed from a portfolio perspective. An alternative approach is to establish a separate portfolio category/segment for mandatory initiatives. Whatever approach is adopted, claims of meeting mandatory requirements should not just be accepted at face value – there should be adequate review to ensure that the requirement is indeed mandatory and the planned response is proportionate and cost-effective.

In some portfolio management environments, prioritization can be a highly complex and mathematical process – for example, where the analytical hierarchy process is used, by which strategic objectives are weighted using pair-wise comparisons (as was introduced in section 4.5) and the strategic contribution of each initiative to each objective is then rated from none to extreme.[34] Such calculations are aided by the use of relevant software tools. However, for the purposes of this guide the key concepts will be discussed using simplified examples that can be adapted to suit any organization. It should also be noted that this is an area where sophisticated approaches are not necessarily more reliable than simple ones – there is always the risk of spurious accuracy. Ultimately, there is no replacement for management judgement, although an objective approach to prioritization can help managers make more informed, consistent and transparent decisions.

A simple approach to prioritization is as follows:

1   Decide on the prioritization criteria that represent the factors the organization views as most important when considering an investment.

Example: Prioritization – keeping it simple and relevant[35]

In order to make a measured and balanced judgement on the correct portfolio content, HMRC determined a set of benefit categories and prioritized them according to Treasury priorities. These categories included tax yield, staffing headcount reductions, customer benefits and cost savings. By taking these elements into account across the portfolio options, and by mapping the time and cost of delivering these benefits from a range of possible programmes and projects, HMRC arrived at an optimum affordable portfolio.

Simple tools were developed to allow the implications of each portfolio option to be clearly understood and avoid too much complexity and automation that could mask real-world issues and decision implications from the portfolio governance committees.

2   Agree the importance of each criterion by assigning a weighting or percentage of relative importance – and ensure that the total percentages of all criteria add up to 100.

3   Agree a rating system to apply to the initiatives – a simple approach is based on 'no contribution' (0), 'some contribution' (5) and 'highest contribution' (10).

4   Rate each change initiative using the ratings and weightings identified above. Total weighted scores can then be divided by the required funding to provide a score per £/$/€ invested. Alternatively, the scale of budget can be represented on a portfolio map via the size of the 'bubble' as shown in Figure 6.5.

5   Collate all prioritization information and analyse – including by using a portfolio map to communicate the findings.

Decision-conferencing approaches have been found to be particularly effective in such situations. Here senior management debate and agree the relative importance of the strategic objectives, the criteria to be used to assess strategic contribution and the scores/ratings for each initiative. The role of the facilitator can be crucial in ensuring that differences of perception are debated openly and a consensus is reached. The advantages of decision-conferencing include improved commitment by senior management both to the success of the portfolio and to portfolio management itself.

Table 6.5 Example – scoring a proposed change initiative using weighted prioritization criteria

		Contribution				
	Weight	None	Some	High	Score	Total
Prioritizing change criteria						
1 Supports at least one strategic objective	20%	0	5	10	10	2
2 Realizes significant benefits in a short time with low risk	20%	0	5	10	5	1
3 Contributes to external targets	10%	0	5	10	0	0
4 Complies with a legislative requirement	25%	0	5	10	10	2.5
5 Addresses an area of underperformance	5%	0	5	10	5	0.25
6 Improves efficiency	5%	0	5	10	5	0.25
7 Mitigates against corporate risk	10%	0	5	10	10	1
8 Honours an existing contractual obligation	5%	0	5	10	10	0.5
				Change priority score		7.5

Table 6.6 Example – ranked list of change initiatives

Priority	Change name	Budget	Benefit	Risk	Priority score
1	Proposed change 2	£5.1 m	H	H	10
2	Proposed change 6	£1.6 m	H	M	10
3	Proposed change 5	£4.1 m	H	M	10
4	Proposed change 1	£1.1 m	M	M	7.5
5	Proposed change 8	£550 k	M	M	6
6	Proposed change 7	£100 k	M	L	5
7	Proposed change 3	£2.1 m	H	H	2
8	Proposed change 4	£3.1 m	L	H	2

6.4.3 Prioritization – a simplified example

This section provides an example of how change initiatives can be prioritized and how the resulting analyses can then be used to inform senior management decision-making. Table 6.5 shows an example of a proposed change initiative that has been assessed using a simple weighted prioritization scoring mechanism.

When each initiative has been scored as described, the information can be collated into a ranked listing. Sorting by descending priority order provides a clear view on which initiatives are most important to the organization. Table 6.6 illustrates a basic prioritized list.

This analysis can also be enhanced by dividing the priority score by the cost of the initiative – and then listing the change initiatives in order of score per £/$/€ thousand/million invested. This information can also be illustrated in a simple bubble matrix portfolio map as shown in Figure 6.5. Note that the size of the bubble represents the relative size of the budget; and the organization's tolerance to risk is shown by the position of the dotted line.

Immediately, it is clear that change 4 is high-risk and returns low benefits, despite having one of the largest budgets. This initiative should be reviewed to consider whether it should continue (perhaps because it meets some legal or regulatory requirement or enables other higher-priority initiatives) or should be stopped.

The application of prioritization in practice is illustrated by the following examples (also see the Aston Martin example in section 6.5).

Example: Portfolio prioritization in the European Parliament IT portfolio[36]

In addition to segmenting the portfolio as described in section 6.3, potential initiatives in the European Parliament's IT portfolio are assessed using a multi-dimensional framework based on the following transparent and measurable appraisal criteria: criticality, expected business benefits, foreseen business risk, compatibility with the IT systems strategy, request maturity, costs, IT risk and political impact. Each of these criteria is assessed through a number of questions, the answers to which are backed up with satisfactory evidence by request owners and technical assessors.

In this way, a prioritized list of potential initiatives can be obtained by business domain, providing a sound basis for the allocation of funding and human resources. It is also emphasized that, although the prioritization is done by an algorithm, the results are not applied blindly, but pass through the filter of a 'sanity check' review by business users and the IT directorate.

Example: Using portfolio prioritization to achieve best value for money[37]

Each year from 2001 to 2009 the UK Ministry of Defence (MoD) equipment programme required a fair and equitable portfolio prioritization process to achieve best military value for money across the complete equipment portfolio. This portfolio evaluation would be required to accommodate cost savings and enhancement measures for all directorates of equipment capability (DECs) and would use the expertise and experience across the MoD.

Table 6.7 Prioritize: keys to success

Key	Explanation
Tailor the investment criteria	The prioritization criteria should be tailored to the portfolio or portfolio segment's objectives and should reflect both risk/achievability and return/attractiveness dimensions. 'Risk' or 'achievability' includes factors such as reputational risk, technical and project risk, and the probability that benefits will actually be realized in practice. 'Return' or 'attractiveness' includes factors such as 'political' need, financial return and scale of strategic contribution. Finally, such criteria also need to take account of the scale of investment required; e.g. initiative X may have a greater impact than initiative Y, but if it costs twice as much, management will need to consider whether the additional investment is justified by the incremental benefits.
Involve the management board	The management board, PDG or investment committee must agree the prioritization criteria (and any weightings) and are the key decision makers regarding the final prioritized list of change initiatives. Approaches such as decision-conferencing have been found to be very effective not only in reaching consensus over a prioritized portfolio, but also in gaining shared commitment to the portfolio and the portfolio management process itself.
Use multi-criteria analysis	Utilize financial investment criteria (such as NPV, IRR and payback) but also use multi-criteria analysis examining return/attractiveness in the context of risk/achievability.
Use evidence-based assessments	Work through the prioritization criteria for each proposed change initiative – and ensure ratings are evidenced so that it is clear why certain assessments have been made and to provide confidence that all initiatives have been appraised on a level playing field. Use reference class forecasting if the data is available – and if not, start collecting the data.
Be creative in presenting the findings	Be creative with the way findings are presented. Graphical representation, including portfolio maps, can be particularly useful in communicating key messages in a clear and succinct manner.

An open, inclusive approach to corporate portfolio management was employed. Each of the 13 DECs prioritized individual portfolios using decision-conferencing to arrive at a portfolio of options which would deliver the best military capability from the resources available. The process was designed to help the MoD assess relative priority between proposed savings and potential enhancements to address identified capability requirements within the constraints of a limited budget, and also to deliver improved benefits in future military capability within the available resources.

A final decision conference then brought these portfolios together to create an overall portfolio of prioritized programme options for endorsement by the Joint Capability Board.

This final portfolio helped the MoD to align resources across the DECs in accordance with defence strategy, taking into account the necessary trade-offs, and balancing short- and long-term priorities.

An essential and significant part of the overall portfolio management approach was the involvement and engagement of the stakeholders. This was considered especially important when looking at budget cuts, as improving the transparency of the way resources are allocated leads to a greater level of buy-in and a deeper commitment to deliver the final agreed portfolio.

6.5 PORTFOLIO MANAGEMENT PRACTICE 4: BALANCE

6.5.1 What is the purpose?

Prioritization results in a ranked list of strategic changes. The purpose of the 'balance' practice is to ensure that the resulting portfolio is balanced in terms of factors such as timing; coverage of all strategic objectives; impact across the business; stage of initiative development; overall risk:return profile; and available resources.

6.5.2 What is involved?

Whilst some form of balancing occurs throughout the portfolio definition cycle, it is only when the proposed change initiatives have been prioritized that detailed balancing decisions can be made. Balancing concerns ask whether the prioritized list of initiatives is still optimum when taking account of factors such as:

- Timing/scheduling initiatives so that an even manageable spread is achieved and an unsustainable burden is not put on specific parts of the business, which would adversely impact operational performance.
- Delivering all the organization's strategic objectives or adjusting those objectives to match what is achievable and affordable.
- Impact across the business – both by product/service and by geographical area.
- Change initiatives at various stages in their delivery lifecycle – from concept through to implementation.
- High-risk/high-return and low-risk/low-return initiatives.
- Matching supply and demand for constrained resources or arranging to acquire additional resources.

The reality that portfolio management is rarely introduced to a 'greenfield' site, as discussed under the 'understand' practice (see section 6.2.2), also needs to be taken into consideration. For example, the ability to cancel current initiatives can be limited by existing contractual commitments. In such instances, whilst room for manoeuvre may be limited in the short term, making the implications transparent can prompt action to manage such commitments down over time and so gain greater flexibility in resource allocation.

Balancing is not achieved by the portfolio office working in isolation – it needs to collaborate with colleagues in functions such as strategy, HR, PPM, IT and operational management to determine the most appropriate portfolio. This also emphasizes the importance of the portfolio office having no responsibility for initiative delivery (so its analyses are independent and objective) and reporting to the portfolio governance body (so its conclusions are, and are perceived to be, in the interests of the organization as a whole). Once this consultation and analysis phase is completed, the portfolio office should present the proposed balanced portfolio, together with supporting recommendations, to the relevant portfolio governance body – i.e. the management board or PDG/ investment committee.

6.5.3 Being creative to support decision-making

The value added by the portfolio office should include the development of creative and easy-to-understand representations of the balanced portfolio. Sending one spreadsheet to the portfolio governance body will rarely suffice. The portfolio map at Figure 6.5 provides an example of how to graphically represent change initiatives based on budget, risk and benefit data. Another interesting option – the 'Tornado' diagram showing costs and benefits by strategic initiative – is illustrated at Figure 6.6.[38]

Other possible graphical representations include:

- Comparisons of demand and supply for constrained resources showing under/over allocations
- Share of investment by portfolio category/ segment
- Scale of investment by strategic objective
- Anticipated benefits by business area
- Coverage by strategic objective and timing
- Business value and criticality matrix
- Criticality and complexity matrix
- Value and cost matrix
- Analysis of coverage by portfolio category and area of the business
- A dependencies map – showing where major dependencies exist between initiatives (see also section 7.5.3).

The output from this analysis will be a report to the portfolio governance body, which enables them to consider, revise if necessary, and then approve the proposed portfolio – this is addressed under the plan practice below (section 6.6).

Important note

Portfolio and programme management software packages can be extremely useful when balancing because they enable a range of constraints to be added and changed to suit the organization and undertake 'what if?' analyses. Provided that the software has been configured correctly and is populated with reliable information, the analyses available can inform portfolio balancing.

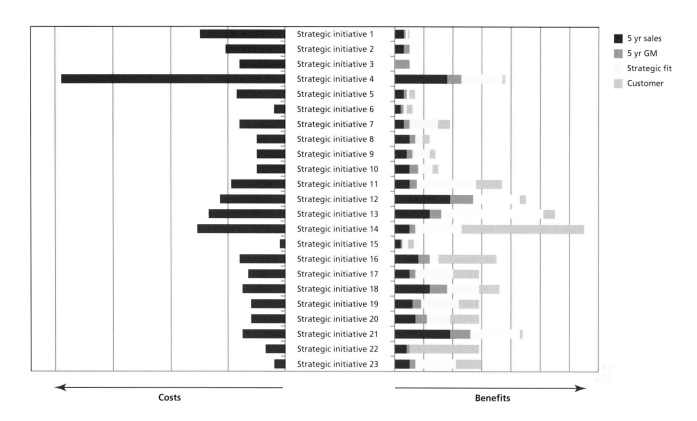

Figure 6.6 'Tornado' diagram. Note that GM stands for gross margin, and the customer rating refers to the scale of customer demand.

Table 6.8 Balance: keys to success

Key	Explanation
Ensure that balance follows understanding, categorization and prioritization	Some form of balancing occurs throughout the portfolio definition cycle. However, it is most powerful when the understand, categorize and prioritize practices have been completed.
Set the expectations of the portfolio governance body	Ensure that the portfolio governance body (portfolio direction group/investment committee or equivalent) understands its role in balancing the portfolio, the information it will receive and the decisions it will be required to make.
Consult widely	The portfolio office must ensure appropriate consultation with relevant functions across the organization when balancing the portfolio, including strategic planning, PPM and performance management.
Present findings creatively	Present findings and information in creative and easily understandable graphical formats. The information should be summarized but enable drill-down to key information when required.
Evidence findings	Ensure that recommendations such as stopping or re-scoping a programme or project are justified with facts so that everyone understands the rationale for such decisions.
Exercise discretion	Where initiatives are recommended for de-prioritization, careful handling is required. People may have invested time and emotional energy in getting the initiative to where it is today and may therefore perceive de-prioritization as personal criticism. Portfolio office staff consequently need well-developed soft skills including tact and diplomacy.
Use analyses to inform decision-making	Algorithms, decision rules and investment criteria can guide decision-making, but ultimately what initiatives are included in the portfolio rely on senior management judgement.

Example: Balancing the portfolio[39]

The scenario

The IT portfolio of an organization, as with all portfolios, needs to be appropriate for that organization's aims, size and capability. Aston Martin, a successful and globally known manufacturer of high-quality motor cars, recognized this as one of its major opportunities.

The business had come under new ownership giving it significant flexibility – particularly in relation to its IT systems and processes, which had previously been predominantly mandated by its parent company. Due to the aggressive time constraints that were agreed for the separation from the previous holding company, many of the fixes that were implemented to maintain business continuity were not optimized and this, coupled with a historical lack of investment within IT, meant that many issues were beginning to surface, exposing the company to significant business risk.

The company had a state-of-the-art manufacturing facility; but its IT operations were fairly archaic. It had been relying on the same company-wide software system that had been in use for 25 years. IT, split across two sites, had about 50 people – a sizable number considering the overall size of the entire organization. Plus, it was working on numerous projects, typically prioritized by the age-old method: 'whoever shouts the loudest'. There were at least three times more projects requiring delivery than the available budget or resources to support them.

The response

The company had a very clear strategy and an aligned set of business drivers. The IT function therefore started developing a set of strategic drivers that, while being IT specific, aligned directly to the overall company strategy. A critical part of the process was gaining agreement from all the project sponsors (mostly at board level) that the strategic drivers and associated priorities were correct. This paid dividends later in the process when justifying to the project sponsors where their specific projects ranked in relation to others.

The inventory for all the projects within the portfolio was collated, amassing as much information about each project as possible. This included details of resource requirements, potential business benefits and of course financial data.

Every project within the portfolio was then assessed in terms of its:

- Ability to deliver against the defined IT business drivers and so achieve 'strategic value'.
- Maturity in relation to a set of predefined set of questions relating to its governance, planning maturity, business benefits, resource requirements and cost.

This resulted in a score for each project to indicate the 'risk' associated with its delivery. Once the portfolio appraisal was complete, the prioritization and balancing, or optimization, could begin.

Balancing the portfolio

By plotting each project on a graph of 'strategic value' against 'risk' (see Figure 6.7) it was clear to see which projects should be invested in and which projects should be parked. The first cut refined the portfolio by dropping the 'obvious' poorly aligned or high-risk projects. The real refinements then came for the borderline projects. These could be 'tuned' by changing scope to add greater strategic value or reduced in risk by investing more effort in planning or resourcing. The portfolio was also used to optimize the available resource pool, identifying abundant skill sets and shortages for the selected projects.

The resulting analysis became a powerful tool for the new chief information officer (CIO) during cost-benefit discussions along the lines of, 'Here's what you get for your £x million. If you want to spend £y million, we can add these projects ...' This entire process took less than 90 days, and while more time could have been spent refining the business cases for each project and planning the delivery schedules in more detail, the 80:20 rule provided enough guidance to make the difficult decisions quickly using enough information to be logical and defendable.

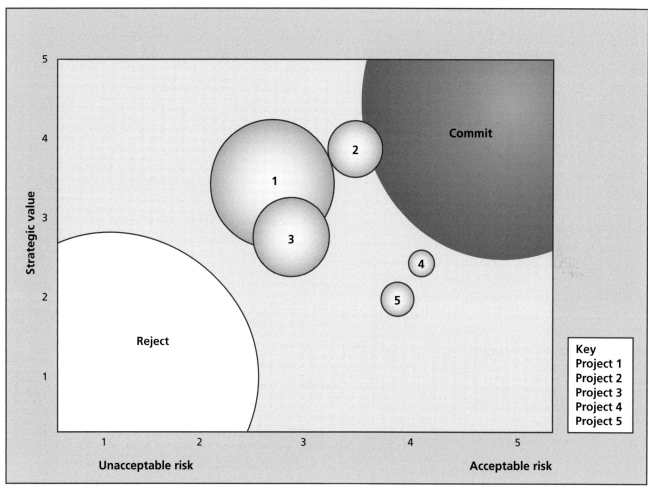

Figure 6.7 Portfolio map and balancing

Other organizations could duplicate this experience in similar timescales depending on the complexity and number of projects to be analysed. Whether an organization is struggling to focus on strategic value or needs to trim costs and projects but doesn't know where to begin, a 'lite' touch to portfolio management enables streamlining of operations in a methodical, meaningful and defendable way. Ultimately, this particular portfolio was balanced to align with the budget and resources available, the strategic drivers and an acceptable level of risk, so providing the CIO with confidence that he was focusing limited investment exactly where it was needed most. Bradley Yorke-Biggs, director of IT and business strategy, concludes, 'Portfolio management has helped shape the foundation of the future IT function within Aston Martin. It has provided me with the confidence that my investment is focused exactly where it is needed.'

6.6 PORTFOLIO MANAGEMENT PRACTICE 5: PLAN

6.6.1 What is the purpose?

The purpose of the 'plan' practice is to collate information from the portfolio definition cycle and create a portfolio strategy and delivery plan which will be approved by the portfolio direction group/ investment committee. The portfolio strategy is a tool to help stakeholders understand what the portfolio is designed to achieve in the longer term (linked to the strategic planning cycle) and provide a high-level overview of how these objectives will be achieved. The portfolio delivery plan in contrast provides a more detailed understanding of the shorter term (usually annual) delivery schedule, cost and resource allocations, and the benefits to be realized. The delivery plan also provides the baseline against which performance will be tracked and reported in the year using the portfolio dashboard report (see section 7.2.2.3).

6.6.2 What is involved?

The portfolio strategy and delivery plan can be combined in a single document or be prepared as separate documents. In either case the objectives are to:

- Provide a longer-term overview, linked to the strategic planning cycle, of the portfolio and what it is designed to achieve, as well as the means by which the objectives will be achieved (the portfolio strategy).
- Provide clarity to all stakeholders with regard to the scope and content of the portfolio (strategy and the delivery plan).
- Motivate people to commit to the delivery of shared goals (both the strategy and the delivery plan).

- Convert the balanced portfolio approved by the relevant portfolio governance body into a plan, usually for the year ahead, with clear milestones, a profiled budget, portfolio-level benefits realization plan, resource schedule and summary of current risks and issues (the portfolio delivery plan).
- Provide a baseline against which progress can be monitored, reviewed and managed via the portfolio dashboard (the portfolio delivery plan).

The portfolio strategy and delivery plan will normally be updated on at least an annual basis by the portfolio office working in close collaboration with the strategy, finance and performance management functions to ensure that they are consistent with the wider organizational strategic, business and financial plans. The portfolio strategy and delivery plan should be presented by the

Table 6.9 Plan: keys to success

Key	Explanation
Summarize the results of the portfolio definition cycle in a portfolio strategy and delivery plan	The portfolio strategy and delivery plan are the main outputs from the portfolio definition cycle. It is critical that everyone understands their purpose and importance.
Provide a clear line of sight	The size and format of the portfolio strategy and delivery plan are irrelevant – the value that they should provide to all stakeholders is not. They should provide a clear view on: ■ What initiatives are included in the portfolio ■ Scheduling/timing of initiatives ■ Resource and financial requirements ■ Key milestones ■ Risks ■ The benefits to be realized. Most significantly of all, they should provide a clear view of the contribution the portfolio will make to the strategic objectives and how this will be measured. The delivery plan also provides the baseline against which portfolio progress can be monitored and managed in the year via the portfolio dashboard report.
The portfolio office prepares the strategy and plan	The portfolio office should lead on the creation of the portfolio strategy and delivery plan, ensuring that colleagues in functions such as strategy, performance management and finance are engaged in their development and understand the implications for their plans.
The portfolio governance body endorses the strategy and plan	The management board or portfolio direction group/investment committee must formally approve the portfolio strategy and delivery plan – and the resource allocations implied.
Keep it simple	Although the portfolio strategy and delivery plan represent a complex planning and delivery environment, they need to be relatively simple, otherwise there is a risk of confusing and alienating stakeholders. So apply the 80:20 or Pareto rule and focus on the most important data, e.g. delivery of those milestones that can affect overall portfolio delivery and the overall benefits to be realized.

business change or portfolio director to the portfolio direction group/investment committee for approval.

Appendix E includes an outline of the contents of the portfolio strategy and delivery plan.

Example: Portfolio delivery plan

One major portfolio introduced an annual portfolio delivery planning process. This process encompassed:

- A review coordinated by the portfolio office of progress to date in terms of spend against budget, meeting key milestones and benefits realized against forecast.
- A review of continued strategic alignment.
- Options for meeting any pressures.

This was summarized in a 20-page document, which provided a basis for senior management re-approval of the portfolio. The portfolio delivery plan was then completed with summaries of the key milestones, cost profile and benefits realization plan for the forthcoming year. This then provided the baseline against which progress was monitored on a monthly basis via the portfolio dashboard report.

Portfolio delivery cycle: practices 6–12

7

7 Portfolio delivery cycle: practices 6–12

7.1 PURPOSE OF THIS CHAPTER

This chapter provides a more detailed discussion of the practices found within the portfolio delivery cycle:

- Management control
- Benefits management
- Financial management
- Risk management
- Stakeholder engagement
- Organizational governance
- Resource management.

For ease of reading, each practice is described by answering the following two questions:

- What is the purpose?
- What is involved?

Real-life examples are included to illustrate the application of these practices – although they should be adapted to suit the specific organizational circumstances.

Keys to success for each of the seven practices discussed in this chapter are given in Tables 7.2, 7.4, 7.5 and 7.7–7.10, respectively.

Two points must be emphasized – firstly, a common theme throughout the practices outlined in this chapter is the need for corporate standards consistent with recognized good practice (such as those contained in the OGC's Best Management Practice guidance). These standards need to be embedded and applied consistently across the organization and in particular within all the programmes and projects, otherwise benefits, costs, risks etc. will not be identified, managed and reported on a like-for-like basis at the portfolio level. The challenge facing the portfolio office is not only to define such standards but to ensure that everyone understands and applies them.

Secondly, the portfolio delivery cycle mirrors the perspectives in P3M3; thus the two are inextricably linked and P3M3 can be used to assess how well these practices are integrated into, and operate effectively within, an organization.

7.2 PORTFOLIO MANAGEMENT PRACTICE 6: MANAGEMENT CONTROL

7.2.1 What is the purpose?

Once agreed, the portfolio strategy and delivery plan form the baseline for what is to be delivered. The purpose of the management control practice is to ensure that progress, at an individual and portfolio level, is regularly monitored against this baseline. This helps to ensure that delivery stays on track and that the portfolio remains strategically aligned.

7.2.2 What is involved?

Management control encompasses five main elements:

- Defined processes, including the business change lifecycle, which should be recorded in a portfolio management framework.
- Guidance and templates for business case preparation, initiative planning etc.
- Regular progress-reporting, including via the portfolio dashboard.
- Stage or phase gates. These include end-of-tranche programme reviews and are in addition to external processes such as the OGC Gateway Reviews.
- Regular portfolio-level reviews.

7.2.2.1 Defined processes including the business change lifecycle

Central to the management control practice are:

- A business change lifecycle, which is used to control the delivery of all change initiatives in the portfolio (or separate lifecycles for the different categories of initiative).
- Escalation procedures for such matters as risks and issues; alterations to schedules; budget variations; and changes to benefits forecast beyond delegated levels. Escalation is usually linked to control limits for spend and schedule, and benefits beyond which variances from plan are referred to the relevant portfolio governance body for approval or remedial action. This in turn facilitates a policy of management by exception as outlined in section 7.2.2.3.

Example: Business change lifecycle

The example of a business change lifecycle illustrated in Figure 7.1 has been successfully rolled out within the Highways Agency where it is called the project control framework. While the Highways Agency uses this for every project, many organizations have a similar approach (some significantly more complex) that can be used for all programmes and projects.

Controlling such processes can be extremely complex and this is why the portfolio office should provide and facilitate training in, and awareness of, the business change lifecycle processes. Consideration should also be given to adopting a champion–challenger model whereby everyone is expected to comply with the defined portfolio processes (the current 'champion' process), but everyone is also encouraged to recommend alternatives or improvements (i.e. 'challengers'). Once adopted, the 'challenger' becomes the new 'champion' process. This not only helps to ensure that processes adapt to lessons learned, but it also encourages stakeholders to engage actively in the portfolio management processes.

Appropriate arrangements should also be established to provide assurance that defined processes are operating as intended. This includes the stage/phase gates and portfolio-level reviews addressed below, and the portfolio office will also need to consider what other mechanisms are appropriate such as those illustrated by the following example on delivery assurance.

Example: Delivery assurance[40]

To underpin effective delivery assurance, HMRC has established two key working groups. The first of these is the Joint Assurance Forum (JAF). This brings together representatives from across the department's assurance provider community, enabling them to exchange planning information and discuss the scope for improving the quality and cost-effective delivery of assurance services to programme and project customers. Members routinely share plans to enhance and refine their individual assurance operations, thereby eliminating redundant processes and removing duplication. JAF also benefits from the regular attendance of colleagues from OGC who provide updates on central assurance initiatives and emerging good-practice proposals.

Coupled to this, HMRC established a Programme Assurance Special Interest Group (PASIG). This aims to promote the development of assurance functions within programmes and to encourage them to build and maintain effective and workable assurance plans that will strengthen programme governance. PASIG meets quarterly and its members are drawn from across the portfolio. As well as an effective forum for promoting good assurance practice, PASIG also benefits from contributions from OGC and input from leaders of change initiatives across the department, providing a broad range of relevant expertise and advice.

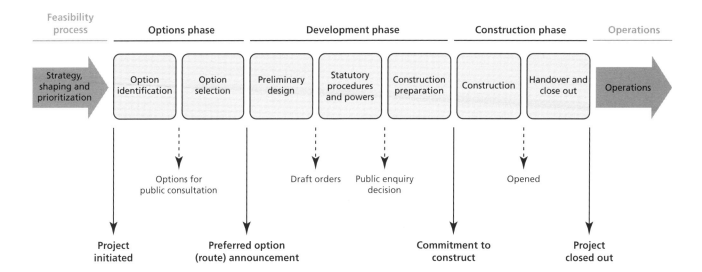

Figure 7.1 Example of a business change lifecycle

The portfolio management, governance and assurance processes should be documented in a portfolio management framework. This provides a central authoritative source of guidance on the way the portfolio is managed, how (and where) decisions are made and on what basis. The portfolio management framework should be placed on the corporate intranet as a central reference point for guidance on the operation of the portfolio.

7.2.2.2 Business case guidance and templates

The effectiveness of a business change lifecycle is enhanced by the use of consistent standards to be followed by all initiatives in the portfolio. This includes ensuring that business cases[41] are created for each initiative and on a consistent basis – this enables strategic contribution to be assessed and initiatives compared on a level playing field. This is also facilitated by the use of standard templates for the main PPM documentation including:

- Project/programme initiation documents
- Concept/feasibility studies
- Strategic, outline and full business cases – and guidance on the detail required at each stage of development
- Benefits management strategy, realization plan and benefit profiles
- Post-implementation review reports.

Informed investment and portfolio prioritization decisions are dependent on accurate and reliable data. A consistent business case template can help, but consideration also needs to be given to the reliability of forecasts of cost, benefit and time to complete the initiative. Research has shown that forecasters tend to underestimate costs and time required and to overestimate the benefits that will be realized. This can be due to the problems of forecasting an uncertain future; simple over-confidence or deliberate misstatement to ensure funding. Whatever the cause, solutions include:

- Adjusting forecasts for optimism bias – for example, the HMT *Green Book* includes standard adjustments to be made to forecasts for different categories of programme and project.
- Adopting in a similar approach what is called **reference class forecasting** whereby forecasts are informed by the organization's track record in delivery, or the experience of others

Example: Reliable business cases

Sound business cases are one of the bedrocks on which effective portfolio management is built as they provide the basis for informed investment appraisal and portfolio prioritization. As part of their approach, American Express[42] developed an investment decision-making guide entitled *Six Steps to Better Decision-making*. This provided a consistent basis for business case preparation and included:

1 State a compelling business case including:

- At a strategic level, how the change will lead to competitive advantage.
- At a tactical level, sufficient detail to understand how it will be achieved and what risks are involved.

2 Use realistic assumptions based on rigorous analysis, past experience and peer comparisons

3 Build a sound driver-based model and projections.

4 Apply consistent decision-making criteria encompassing financial metrics (NPV, IRR etc.) and measures of strategic contribution.

5 Secure appropriate approvals – the approvals process should be cross-functional to ensure ownership and appropriate scrutiny prior to release of funding.

6 Conduct a thorough post-implementation review – capture lessons learned and apply them in future business cases and investment appraisals..

in delivering similar types of initiative. Data captured as part of post-implementation reviews can in this way help to ensure that lessons learned are applied going forward. This also encourages more reliable forecasting, which in turn means more informed and reliable investment appraisal and portfolio prioritization.

- Defining common frameworks for costing and benefits estimating.
- The use of three-point (optimistic, pessimistic and most likely) rather than single-point estimating.
- Independent validation of estimates – for example, cost estimates may be reviewed by the finance department and benefits forecasts should be agreed with the relevant business representatives.

- Staged release of funding linked to stage/phase gates – in this way, the organization's commitment of resources is linked to confidence in the reliability of the forecasts supplied.
- Summary investment appraisal templates can also add value in making the investment rationale transparent by summarizing the key data under the headings of:
  - Attractiveness (return) e.g. financial return on investment, measure of strategic contribution, benefits etc.
  - Achievability (risk), e.g. delivery confidence assessment, likelihood of benefits realization etc.
  - Affordability both in capital and operating expenditure terms.

This allows senior managers to obtain a quick overview of all portfolio initiatives without having to read a series of lengthy business cases. A sample template from the P3O online repository[43] is shown at Table 7.1.

7.2.2.3 Regular progress reporting

The portfolio office will coordinate progress/highlight reporting from each of the change initiatives on a regular basis (usually at least monthly) and collate this information for the portfolio governance bodies in the form of a dashboard report, which tracks performance against the baseline represented by the portfolio delivery plan. As such the dashboard report should include:

- Progress information against key milestones.
- Status on key initiatives, risks, issues and dependencies.
- Spend and revised forecast compared with the profiled budget.
- The latest benefits forecast and realization to date compared with the plan.

Portfolio management is, however, more than monitoring programme and project progress at an individual level. It also requires that progress is monitored at a portfolio level, investigating whether the organization is delivering as planned; how well programme and project management is performing; whether resources and dependencies are being effectively managed; and whether benefits are being realized. The dashboard report should therefore also include a suite of portfolio-level performance metrics encompassing both lead and outcome indicators (see Appendix F).

Portfolio management provides the information to enable action to be taken to address delivery issues on poorly performing but strategically necessary programmes and projects. Indeed, it can also enable proactive action to prevent such problems – one of the functions of the portfolio office is to monitor progress with a view to identifying constraints that could impact on delivery and then recommend appropriate action to mitigate this risk by re-scheduling delivery, acquiring additional resources etc. See sections 7.5.3 and 7.8.

Any decisions required arising from the dashboard report should be highlighted by the portfolio office for management attention. In this way the dashboard provides the portfolio governance bodies with a clear view on progress and performance – and a prompt to management action where intervention is required. This is helped where a policy of management by exception is applied; i.e. only variances that exceed pre-set control limits (for example, +/– 10%) are flagged up for consideration and action by the relevant governance body.

It is emphasized that portfolio reporting will only be valuable if there is confidence in the information, and this is directly related to the quality of information provided by the programmes and projects, e.g. in their highlight reports. Addressing this is aided by the publication of a clear reporting schedule and a policy of one version of the truth – i.e. all reporting of progress should be via the documented route and schedule.

Ultimately, the objective of monitoring and reporting progress is to ensure that the portfolio delivers the planned contribution to strategic objectives. This means that, occasionally, tough decisions may need to be made on whether funding should be maintained for certain programmes and projects. The NAO have, however, reported[44] that according to non-executive directors, whilst senior management increasingly have access to the necessary information to reallocate resources, too often the difficult decision is not made. The use of control limits and management by exception can help by focusing attention on material variances from plan. The roles of the portfolio office, business change/portfolio director and non-executive directors are

Table 7.1 Example of an investment appraisal template

Project name:				Business sponsor:	
Management summary					
Financial appraisal summary					

Cash flow	Expenditure			Savings	Cumulative cash flow
	Capital	Non-capital	Total		
Year 0					
Year 1					
Year 2					
Year 3					
Totals					

Benefits (£)			
Payback period			
Net present value (NPV)			
Internal rate of return (IRR)			
Return on investment (ROI)			
Resource type	Internal (days)	External (days)	Total

Strategic attractiveness summary		
	Weighting	Score
Strategic alignment		
Confidence in benefits analysis		
Clarity of objectives		
Buy-in of stakeholders		
Attractiveness total		
Achievability summary		
	Weighting	Score
Complexity		
Capability		
Ownership and accountability		
Belief of stakeholders in achievability		
Achievability total		

also important in ensuring that portfolio reporting does not become a box-ticking exercise and that, where required, the tough decisions are made. The key questions to ask are does the portfolio dashboard report provide a clear line of sight from planning to performance, and is it used on an *active* basis to drive improved performance? This should be assessed as part of the periodic review of portfolio effectiveness referred to below in section 7.2.2.5.

An example of a dashboard report from the P3O online repository[45] is shown in Figure 7.2.

One final comment – fitting all relevant information on a single-page portfolio dashboard report can prove problematic. One approach is to adopt a series of single-page reports (tailored to the local circumstances) – for example, for:

- Portfolio-level spend against profiled budget
- Progress on key milestones compared to schedule
- Benefits realized compared to forecast.

An example of an extract from a portfolio dashboard report focusing on delivery assessment in the Home Office[46] is shown at Figure 7.3.

> **Important note**
>
> When designing the portfolio management reporting process, ensure that the portfolio governance body which will receive the report is consulted on the content and format of the report. Similarly, ensure that those who will provide data for the report understand the data required and the schedule for reporting.

7.2.2.4 Stage/phase ('go'/'no go') gates

The business change lifecycle will specify the points at which initiatives should be reviewed for continued business justification. This should be in addition to external reviews such as the OGC Gateway Reviews which report to the SRO. Referred to here are periodic reviews of initiatives at key points in the project or programme lifecycle – for example, one approach would be to mirror the OGC gateways: business justification,

Portfolio indicators

(R) ⇔ **Benefits realization** – 20/130 projects' benefits at risk ($20m)	(A) ⇧ **Risk** – 20/130 projects not managing risks effectively	(A) ⇩ **Time** – 90/130 projects behind schedule
(R) ⇧ **Budget** – 20/130 projects over budget ($10m at risk)	(A) ⇩ **Resource** – 10/130 projects are short of critical resources	(G) ⇔ **Embedding change** – 30/130 projects are following the project mgmt standards

Consolidated and analysed

Project indicators

1 Management and control (i.e. how well the project is being managed, project health)

2 Actual performance/delivery (i.e. how well the project is delivering benefits)

Name	ID	Type	Priority	Project owner	Business unit owner	Stage gate	1 Management and control: This mth	1 Management and control: Last mth	2 Delivery: This mth	2 Delivery: Last mth	Notes	Finish date	R
Project 1	11	Efficiency	1	B Wilson	Div C	Deploy	R ⇩	A	A ⇩	G	PM not allocated since last month's request	Feb-11	✔
Project 2	21	Compliance	3	F Petrou	Div B	PIR	A ⇧	R	G ⇧	A	Critical systems issue addressed	Jun-09	✔
Project 3	35	Revenue	2	P Ternouth	Div A	Initiate	A ⇔	A	A ⇔	A	Reporting not improved since last month, review scheduled	Mar-10	✘

The project's alignment to agreed strategic drivers

Force ranking of project priority against strategic drivers, complexity (risk) and planned benefits

Key project ownership information

Summary of how well the project complies with embedded project management standards e.g. schedule, risk, quality etc.

Summary of the actual status of the project compared to its approved plans as at the reporting date. For example:
- actual progress against planned schedule
- actual spend against planned budget (and use of contingency)
- benefits realization progress
- level of risk

Has reporting been submitted on time and to the required quality?

Figure 7.2 Example of a portfolio dashboard report

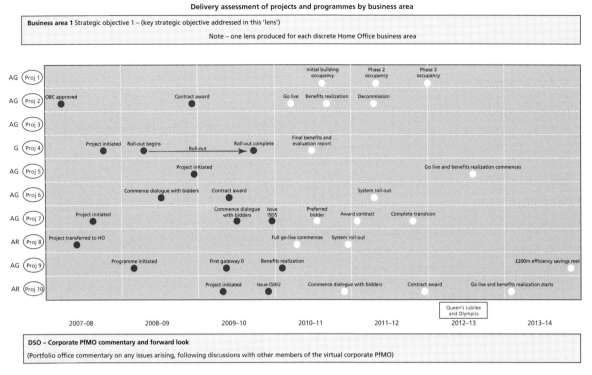

Figure 7.3 Home Office portfolio dashboard delivery assessment

procurement strategy, investment decision, readiness for service and benefits evaluation. Crucially, staged release of funding should be linked to these stage/phase gates so that resource allocation is linked to assessment of performance and continued strategic alignment.

Particular attention should be given to a start gate to ensure that entry to the portfolio is strictly controlled and that significant sums of money are not invested before initial review for consistency with the existing portfolio.

7.2.2.5 Portfolio-level reviews

In addition to regular review of individual initiatives, the portfolio as a whole should be reviewed on a regular basis – every six months is sufficient for most organizations, or for larger portfolios this can take place annually during the updating of the portfolio strategy and delivery plan. Such reviews should encompass:

- Progress to date against the portfolio strategy and delivery plan in terms of:
  - Is delivery on schedule, are key milestones being met and are limited resources and dependencies being effectively managed?
  - Spend against profiled budget and forecast outturn.
  - Benefits realized compared to plan (including impact on the BAU KPIs).

- Performance against the portfolio-level performance metrics.
- Progress looking forward:
  - Are the initiatives included in the portfolio strategy and delivery plan still necessary and sufficient in relation to the current strategic objectives?
  - What degree of confidence is appropriate that the portfolio strategy and delivery plan will be achieved?

In addition to assessing the performance of the portfolio, the review should also assess how well the portfolio management processes are working – for example, are initiatives progressing through the business change lifecycle sufficiently quickly; are defined processes being complied with; are stakeholders actively engaged; and are the defined processes adapted in the light of lessons learned from post-implementation reviews and submissions using the champion–challenger model? This review can be informed by the completion of the health check assessment at Appendix A by senior managers – and analysis of the results to assess to what extent there is a shared view and the trend in the assessments.

Further guidance on measuring portfolio performance is contained in Appendix F.

Example: An effective gateway process[47]

A significant proportion of Peterborough City Council's expenditure is through programmes and projects, and it is important that this investment is directed at the right issues and community needs, and that the projects undertaken are robustly planned and delivered. The Peterborough City Council (PCC) gateway process is based on the Office of Government Commerce (OGC) gateway process and is coordinated by the programme and project management team. It is designed to provide a suitable level of assurance and guidance to help ensure success. The gateway process consists of four distinct gateways (see Figure 7.4) and it examines programmes and projects at key decision points in their lifecycle, giving confidence that they can progress successfully to the next stage. This gateway system provides:

- Assurance on delivering strategic ambitions and alignment of investment to outcomes within the sustainable community strategy
- Assurance that project delivery will take place and not require additional funding
- An audit trail of project activity
- A means to improve risk and issue management
- A means to embed effective and consistent programme and project management methodologies across the organization
- Improved success in delivering project outcomes and realizing benefits
- Streamlined processes, ensuring consistency and clarity of expectations
- Documentation and information that is scaled appropriately to the size and complexity of a project
- A focus on stopping projects at appropriate times.

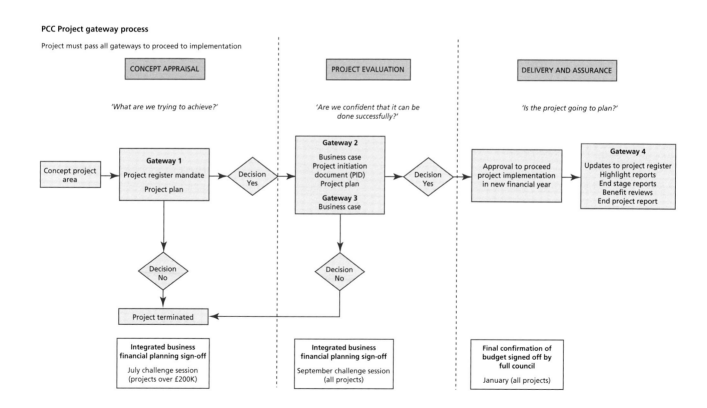

Figure 7.4 Peterborough City Council's gateway process

Table 7.2 Management control: keys to success

Key	Explanation
An effective business change lifecycle	Implement a standard business change lifecycle, encompassing regular stage/phase gates at key points in the programme or project lifecycle.
Clearly understood processes	Ensure that key stakeholders are aware of what is expected of them: ■ Provide ongoing training and awareness sessions on the business change lifecycle, business case standards etc. ■ Record the portfolio management processes and governance in the portfolio management framework and make it available via the corporate intranet.
Reliable forecasting	Track initiative performance via robust post-implementation reviews and use reference class forecasting and optimism bias adjustments to improve the accuracy and reliability of initiative forecasts.
A summary investment appraisal template	Implement a standard summary investment appraisal template to capture the salient data on attractiveness, achievability and affordability.
Staged release of funding	Implement staged release of funding – linking continued funding for initiatives to assessment of performance and continued strategic alignment.
Effective progress reporting	Ensure that regular portfolio progress reporting is effective – design a dashboard report and apply the policies of 'one version of the truth' and management by exception.
Prompt progress reporting	Ensure that programme and project information is presented in a timely manner.
Regular review of performance and continuous improvement	Regularly review the performance of the portfolio as a whole in terms of spend against budget, progress against schedule, and benefits realized against plan. Also assess the performance of the portfolio management processes and whether risk and dependencies are being effectively managed.

7.3 PORTFOLIO MANAGEMENT PRACTICE 7: BENEFITS MANAGEMENT

7.3.1 What is the purpose?

The purpose of the benefits management practice is to clearly identify and manage the benefits being realized from the portfolio, so helping to ensure the best use of available resources and that the contribution to operational performance and strategic objectives is maximized.

7.3.2 What is involved?

Just as MSP recommends that a programme should have a benefits management strategy, so a benefits management framework should be prepared for the portfolio as a whole – and programme-level benefits management strategies should be consistent with it. A portfolio benefits management framework encompasses six main elements: benefits eligibility rules including a consistent approach to benefits categorization; a portfolio-level benefits realization plan; inclusion of re-appraisal of the benefits case at stage/phase gates and portfolio-level reviews; effective arrangements to manage benefits post project/

programme closure; clear arrangements for benefits tracking and reporting at a portfolio level, including via the portfolio dashboard; and regular and robust post-implementation reviews and feeding lessons learned back into forecasting and the benefits management processes. These six elements are considered in turn.

1 Benefits eligibility rules define how benefits should be categorized, quantified, valued and validated in the preparation of relevant initiative documentation, including business cases. This requires a consistent approach to benefits mapping and, ideally, development of a consistent set of metrics to link benefits to strategic objectives (see section 4.5). This then allows change initiatives to be compared on a consistent basis. Central to the portfolio level, benefits eligibility rules are a consistent approach to benefits categorization. Common approaches include:
   - Financial and non-financial benefits
   - Cashable and non-cashable benefits
   - Efficiency/productivity and effectiveness/performance benefits
   - Economy, efficiency and effectiveness benefits.

Further guidance on benefits categorization is contained within MSP – but the key point from a portfolio perspective is that whatever categorization framework is used, it should be applied consistently by all initiatives in the portfolio. This helps to consolidate benefits data and can also help prevent double counting – by ensuring a consistent approach to categorization and quantification, and then by validating these benefits with the relevant business representative. Extracts from the guidelines used by one organization are included at Appendix D, and two examples of benefits categorization are illustrated below.

Example: Benefits categorization for service transformation agreement

The benefits categorization shown in Figure 7.5 was developed for the cross-government service transformation agreement to facilitate consistent and comprehensive benefits forecasts and reporting on benefits realization.

Example: Benefits categorization for the criminal justice system

The criminal justice system (CJS) IT portfolio used an efficiency/effectiveness categorization framework (with sub-categories for cashable and opportunity value benefits) but also enhanced this by analysing which department or criminal justice organization (CJO) would receive the benefit. This can be particularly effective in portfolios that cross organizational boundaries as the process of identifying benefit recipients can help validate forecasts and also lays the basis for their subsequent realization (see Table 7.3).

The following definitions were used:
- **Efficiency benefits**   Savings in staff time, equipment costs etc. Such benefits were further divided into the following sub-categories:
  - **Cashable**   These benefits enable current output to be delivered at lower cost. This includes the additional costs of a policy decision that are avoided due to resource

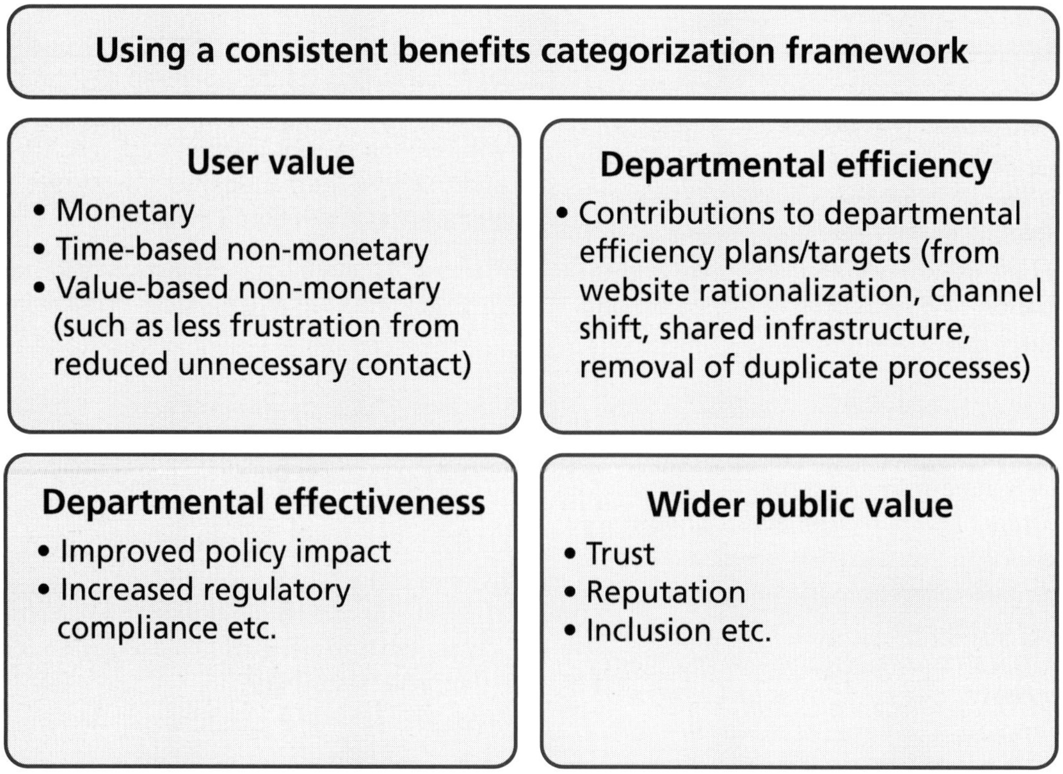

Using a consistent benefits categorization framework

User value
- Monetary
- Time-based non-monetary
- Value-based non-monetary (such as less frustration from reduced unnecessary contact)

Departmental efficiency
- Contributions to departmental efficiency plans/targets (from website rationalization, channel shift, shared infrastructure, removal of duplicate processes)

Departmental effectiveness
- Improved policy impact
- Increased regulatory compliance etc.

Wider public value
- Trust
- Reputation
- Inclusion etc.

Figure 7.5 Service transformation agreement benefits categorization

Table 7.3 Portfolio benefits categorization – CJS IT

Benefit recipient	Benefit type			
	Efficiency		Effectiveness	
	Cashable	Opportunity value	Cashable	Opportunity value
	£	£	£	£
Sponsoring CJO				
Other CJOs				
Other parts of the CJS				
Cross-CJS				
Beyond the CJS				

savings being achieved elsewhere, e.g. productivity savings which enable staff to be re-deployed, thereby removing the need to recruit new staff that would otherwise have been required.

- **Opportunity value/non-cashable** The value of activities that could be undertaken due to productivity improvements that would otherwise not have been undertaken or which would have been completed to a lower standard of quality.

■ **Effectiveness benefits** The economic value (as required by the HMT *Green Book*) assigned to performance improvements. Effectiveness benefits were defined as the impact of addressing the root causes of major problems in the criminal justice system and so contributing to delivery of the strategic vision, public service agreement (PSA) targets, other government priorities and KPIs. The majority of effectiveness benefits were opportunity value. Increased tax or fine revenues did not count as a cashable benefit as they represented a transfer from individuals to the state, but they could be categorized as an effectiveness benefit – e.g. improved rates of fine enforcement.

2   Preparation of a portfolio-level benefits realization plan providing a clear forecast for the forthcoming planning period of the combined impact of current and completed change initiatives on operational performance and strategic objectives – and the metrics that will be used to assess this impact. The portfolio governance body can then come to a view as to whether, in the light of the organization's accumulated investment in change and the benefits realized to date, the

benefits forecast is sufficiently ambitious. Once agreed, the portfolio benefits realization plan, or a summary of it, should be included in the portfolio delivery plan and progress against the plan should be monitored via the dashboard report.

3   A clear commitment to consideration of the updated benefits forecast at each stage/phase gate and portfolio-level review – including what changes in the benefits forecast have occurred, and whether the initiative still represents value for money and a compelling case for investment. All such reviews should include formal re-commitment to realization of the benefits forecast by the relevant SRO and benefits owners.

4   A clear description of how benefits will be managed post programme or project completion and who is responsible for their realization. This is often a real issue in practice – and one that a portfolio approach can address by ensuring continued transparency about benefits beyond initiative closure. It can also help by ensuring that:

- Benefits are consistently expressed in terms that clearly demonstrate the impact on strategic objectives and BAU KPIs.
- Examples of partial whole/full-time equivalent (i.e. part of a person) savings are identified. Such savings can be difficult to realize at a programme or project level, but at a portfolio level the staff time savings from various change initiatives can be combined to identify where staff time can be reallocated to other value-adding activity.
- Unplanned benefits are identified and fully realized across the organization by disseminating examples of good practice.

Example: Portfolio-level benefits management

Ensuring a portfolio-wide, post-programme/project focus on benefits realization can be aided by the nomination of a benefits realization manager in a corporate rather than programme or project position. Within the Driver and Vehicle Licensing Agency (DVLA), a centralized change management team has been established with a remit to:

■ Support projects and operational change teams in ensuring change is relevant and fit for purpose.

■ Ensure consistency of business change approaches across the agency.

■ Ensure business readiness for agency change.

■ Ensure that benefits forecasting and realization is accurate and actually happens.

■ Provide an integrated view of change across the agency.

■ Help, support, understand, advise, represent and make life easier for the business areas.

Significantly, the head of business change management (akin to the business change/portfolio director role shown in Appendix B) monitors and reports on benefits realization and has a seat on all change programme boards.

● The causes of unrealized benefits are effectively addressed.

Ensuring a portfolio-wide, post programme/project focus on benefits realization can be aided by the nomination of a benefits manager at portfolio level. This position may well sit within the portfolio office, and a role description is included in Appendix B.

5 Clear description of the arrangements for benefits tracking and reporting. Benefits information at a portfolio level should be included in the portfolio dashboard including revised forecast and benefits realization to date compared with the benefits realization plan. This assists with decision-making, particularly where delivery slippage occurs as senior management will be able to see the impact

Table 7.4 Benefits management: keys to success

Key	Explanation
Benefits management framework	Ensure that the portfolio benefits management framework includes a set of benefits eligibility rules covering the categorization, quantification, valuation and validation of benefits, and that they are used by all initiatives in the portfolio.
Evidence-based forecasting	Use reference class data from post-implementation reviews to inform benefits forecasting.
Portfolio-level benefits realization plan	Complete a portfolio-level benefits realization plan showing the benefits to be realized in the forthcoming period. The relevant portfolio governance body can then determine whether, in the context of the investment and benefits realized to date, this is sufficiently challenging. This plan also provides the baseline against which progress can be monitored in year.
Ongoing management of benefits	Ensure that benefits management is viewed as a constant throughout the business change lifecycle and not just something that occurs to justify investment in the business case. Revisit the benefits case at every stage/phase gate and portfolio-level review. Ensure an effective oversight of benefits beyond project or programme closure.
Link to portfolio reporting	Include benefits realization in the portfolio dashboard. When initiatives slip, consider the impact on the benefits realization plan, operational performance and strategic objectives – and ensure this is included in reporting to the portfolio governance body.
Post-implementation reviews	Ensure that post-implementation reviews are undertaken and that: ■ Lessons learned are fed back into the benefits management processes. ■ Benefits realized compared to forecast are used to inform forecasting on future initiatives.

on the high-level benefits realization plan and anticipated contribution to strategic targets.

6 Formal post-implementation review – change initiatives should be evaluated after implementation to assess:

- Were forecast benefits realized?
- What unplanned benefits were realized and is there scope to leverage additional benefits?
- Did the initiative represent value for money (i.e. actual costs compared with benefits realized)?
- What lessons can be learned for future change initiatives and to improve the way benefits realization is managed?

This completes the benefits management cycle – as data on benefits realized from the end programme/project and post-implementation reviews (and Gateway 5 reviews) is fed back into the benefits forecasting process – see the discussion of reference class forecasting at section 7.2.2.2.

7.4 PORTFOLIO MANAGEMENT PRACTICE 8: FINANCIAL MANAGEMENT

7.4.1 What is the purpose?

The purpose of the financial management practice is to ensure that the portfolio management processes and decisions are aligned to the financial management cycle and that financial considerations form a key element in all decisions regarding the commencement and ongoing viability of change initiatives, both at an individual and at a collective level.

Important note

Aligning portfolio management with financial management can be challenging. It is critical that the finance department is fully consulted on this. Not only are its staff experts in the financial management processes, but they will also have the best understanding of the potential financial implications of investment decisions.

7.4.2 What is involved?

The importance of aligning portfolio and organizational governance has already been covered in Chapter 3, and this includes aligning portfolio management with the budget allocation process as discussed in section 3.4. Irrespective of which governance structure is adopted, the main elements of portfolio financial management are:

- Selection of appropriate investment criteria including financial metrics such as NPV and hurdle rates of return. Another consideration concerns whether a single set of criteria is used or whether the portfolio is segmented with the investment criteria being tailored to each portfolio segment or category.
- Clear rules for compiling cost forecasts in business cases (in many organizations such forecasts need to be approved by the finance function) and adjusting for optimism bias[48] or the tendency for business case writers to underestimate costs and project duration, and overestimate benefits. This can be achieved via reference class forecasting – adjusting estimates to reflect the organization's track record or the performance of others in delivering similar initiatives.
- Clear rules for valuing efficiency savings and other benefits in business cases – and treatment of cashable benefits – for example, 'booking' them in operational budgets by reducing baselines, headcount limits and target unit costs.
- Clear control limits for reporting variances from budget and approving additional funding requests.
- A financial plan that must be incorporated within every business case. This will include the required capital and operating expenditure to complete the initiative and the consequent financial requirements post implementation – i.e. the financial impact on BAU including depreciation and cost of capital charges where applicable.
- The application of the concept of staged release of funding linked to the stage/phase gates. This helps to ensure that funding allocations remain aligned to strategy and minimizes risk as it facilitates reallocation of funding should that be required. This in turn requires that attention be given to greater use of modular developments addressing number five in the OGC/NAO common causes of project failure – 'Too little attention to breaking development and implementation into manageable steps.' Where this is addressed, wasted expenditure is minimized as resources can more easily be reallocated in response to changed strategic priorities.

- The portfolio delivery plan should include a portfolio-level financial plan showing the profiled capital and operating expenditure budgets in the forthcoming period. The plan should also show in summary the impact on operating expenditure in future years and how any cashable savings are to be re-cycled to fund new initiatives.
- Monitoring spend in the year against the portfolio-level financial plan via the portfolio dashboard.
- Deciding how much financial contingency is retained at a portfolio level to:
  - Address cost escalation on current programmes and projects (where such contingency is retained centrally rather than being included in the individual initiative's budget).
  - Fund new initiatives during the year.

Aligning portfolio management and the organization's financial management processes is particularly valuable because the impact of over/underspends can be recognized early on and managed accordingly – including reallocating emerging underspends to fund new initiatives from the development pipeline. The benefits of integrating portfolio and financial management are illustrated by the Peterborough City Council example.

Example: Portfolio and financial management[49]

At Peterborough City Council, the external auditors noted that the council's use of resources score increased and 'the council has clear financial plans to cope with the impact of the recession. Significant improvements have been made by the council in its financial management arrangements. Financial planning is good. Efficiency savings have been made, helping the council to put more money into areas that residents think are most important. The 'business transformation programme' delivered over £10 million of savings. The council improved its buying arrangements.

7.5 PORTFOLIO MANAGEMENT PRACTICE 9: RISK MANAGEMENT

7.5.1 What is the purpose?

The purpose of the risk management practice is to ensure consistent and effective management of the portfolio's exposure to risk at both individual and collective level. This is crucial to the successful delivery of change initiatives, to delivery of the portfolio as a whole, and ultimately the achievement of the organization's strategic objectives.

Table 7.5 Financial management: keys to success

Key	Explanation
Involve financial experts	Ensure that the portfolio office and finance department work collaboratively. Seconding a finance expert into the portfolio office can be a significant advantage.
Align cycles	Align strategic planning, portfolio management and financial management cycles for optimum value.
Business cases include financial plans completed on a consistent basis	The business change lifecycle should ensure that business cases include a financial plan for every initiative – and these financial plans should be consistent with portfolio-level standards for cost estimation.
Staged release of funding	Incrementally releasing funds in line with the business change lifecycle helps maintain strategic alignment and minimizes the risk of wasted expenditure.
Portfolio-level financial planning	Ensure that a financial plan exists for the portfolio as a whole. This should be included in the portfolio delivery plan.
Regular reporting of progress	Ensure that spend against the portfolio financial plan is included in the portfolio dashboard report. This will require financial reporting information from the change initiatives and the finance system on a regular basis.

7.5.2 What is involved?

Risk management at a portfolio level encompasses the following main elements:

■ Implementing standards which apply to all change initiatives within the portfolio and which align to the organizational risk management policy. A risk management strategy should be agreed at portfolio level and should be included in the portfolio management framework. This risk management strategy should clearly define how and by whom risk is assessed; what criteria are employed in making these assessments; the amount of risk that is to be accepted across the portfolio; tolerance levels for escalation; and reporting processes.

■ Collaborative working with the organizational risk management function which facilitates compliance with organizational policies. Indeed, in some organizations risk management at a portfolio level is carried out by the organizational risk management function. This means that there is no separation between the two and the portfolio is genuinely viewed and managed as a critical element of the business.

■ Incorporating consideration of risk alongside investment return into the portfolio prioritization practice and at each stage/phase gate review.

■ Regular review of risks across the portfolio. The concern here is less about risks and opportunities associated with individual initiatives and more about those risks that run across the portfolio – for example, inaccurate forecasting and variability in returns; slippage on key dependencies; over-exposure to a single supplier; and the negative impact on operational performance of poorly scheduled business change. This in turn requires that the status of such risks is linked to the portfolio risks and issues register, included in the portfolio dashboard report, and also considered as part of the periodic portfolio-level reviews.

■ An effective escalation process that enables risks to be reported to the relevant portfolio governance body.

■ Where appropriate, consideration of risk to the organization from the portfolio – including, for example, financial liabilities associated with performance and guarantee bonds.

■ As mentioned under financial management (see section 7.4), consideration as to whether some budgetary contingency (and if so, how much) should be retained at a portfolio level.

■ Specific consideration of effective management of dependencies across the portfolio – see section 7.5.3.

For more information see *Management of Risk* (M_o_R)[50] and the HM Treasury *Orange Book*.[51]

Example: Portfolio-level risk management

One approach advocated by a US-based portfolio management practitioner group[52] is to adopt a framework for assessing risk across the portfolio encompassing three aspects:

■ Technical risk – i.e. can the programme's or project's technical objectives be achieved?

■ Implementation risk – i.e. can the organization deliver and utilize the technical deliverables? This in part reflects the organization's ability to absorb business change.

■ Commercial or benefit risk – i.e. will the planned strategic, financial or social benefits be realized?

7.5.3 Dependency management

A critical part of any plan at any level – be it project, programme or portfolio – concerns dependencies. Within a simple project this is a relatively easy matter, but in a complex programme or portfolio environment it can be particularly challenging to identify, track and manage dependencies effectively. This is in part because dependencies are not always immediately obvious, but if they are not managed effectively this can represent a serious risk to delivery, and to benefits realization.

The role of the portfolio office is critical in this regard – in ensuring that programme and project planners are aware of, and take into consideration, the scope of all relevant initiatives in the portfolio, and in ensuring dependency information is accurately summarized within the portfolio dashboard report.

Some of the key challenges and sample solutions in dependency management are set out in Table 7.6.

Table 7.6 Key challenges and sample solutions for managing dependencies

Typical dependency management challenges	Sample solutions
Dependency information is not readily available	The portfolio office can organize a workshop to raise awareness of the scope of the portfolio (or specific category/segment) and identification of key dependencies. This can include: ■ Short presentations by each main initiative to summarize the scope and planned business impact of their initiative ■ 1:1 timed sessions where initiatives identify and agree potential dependencies. The results should be consolidated by the portfolio office (e.g. in the form of a dependency matrix as outlined in the example below) and fed back to the participants for validation. This can then inform the dependencies element of the portfolio dashboard.
Uncertainty about what type of dependencies exist	Dependencies include: ■ Where progress on one initiative is dependent on a deliverable from another initiative – i.e. a 'giver'/'receiver' relationship exists. This is a *logical* dependency. ■ Where initiatives are making joint calls on a limited resource (testing resources, facilities, specialist equipment etc.) – i.e. a *logistical* dependency exists. ■ Where realization of benefits from an initiative is dependent on actions beyond the scope of that initiative.
How to document and manage dependencies	There is a wide range of approaches to documenting dependencies. For example, as part of benefits realization management in MSP, outcome relationship modelling is used. In some organizations a central planning software tool can link all dependencies and aggregate the impact on benefits and provide a report automatically. In others, the portfolio office maintains a simple matrix of initiatives with cross-referenced dependencies, and this is updated each month as part of the portfolio progress reporting process. The key point to remember at the portfolio level is to focus on the key dependencies –i.e. those that materially affect the portfolio-level delivery schedule and benefits realization plan.
How to present complex information in an easily understandable form	Dependencies can be represented in a number of ways – for example, in a simple matrix outlined in the example provided, or by highlighting key dependencies on the portfolio schedule. Some organizations link dependencies to the risks and issues register, which can also be incorporated into the monthly reporting cycles.
What are the most important dependencies?	Modify a version of the prioritization practice to focus on dependencies. The portfolio office should work through each dependency and assess which are the most important.

Example: Portfolio-level review of dependencies

Dependency management does not have to mean a sophisticated, bureaucratic, complex approach. One organization adopted a simple matrix with the major change initiatives shown on both the horizontal and vertical axes. The relevant cells in the matrix were then completed to show:

■ Which was the 'giving' and the 'receiving' initiative.

■ A brief description of the dependency and (cross-referenced) key milestone dates.

■ The impact of the dependency on the 'receiving' initiative rated as:
- Mission-critical – slippage on the 'giving' initiative will cause significant slippage on the 'receiving' initiative.
- Major – slippage on the 'giving' initiative will cause slippage on the 'receiving' initiative but this is recoverable – albeit at additional cost.
- Minor – slippage on the 'giving' initiative may have some impact but this is manageable within current resource provision.

Table 7.7 Risk management: keys to success

Key	Explanation
Align the portfolio risk management strategy with the organizational risk management strategy	Standard roles and processes for portfolio risk management should be incorporated into the portfolio management framework. These processes should be consistent with any existing organizational risk management policy.
Involve experts	Ensure close working relationships between the portfolio office and the organizational risk management function where one exists.
Risk-based prioritization	During portfolio prioritization ensure that risk is included as a factor in the prioritization criteria. Use of a matrix highlighting risk (or achievability) and benefit (or attractiveness) is a helpful way to present portfolio-level prioritization data.
Incorporate risk into the business change lifecycle	The management of risk must be embedded within the business change lifecycle. Risks must be owned at an appropriate level and incorporated into the portfolio reporting, reviews and stage/phase gates.
Portfolio risks	A key purpose of portfolio risk management is to oversee the overall level of risk exposure. It is rarely a single risk that will cause major problems but the combination/aggregation of a number of risks that requires the attention of the portfolio office. Focus on both: ▪ Aggregated programme and project risk – such as those relating to ineffective dependency management, over-reliance on a single supplier and the negative impact on operational performance of poorly scheduled change. ▪ Generic risks – for example, those arising from inaccurate forecasting such as delayed delivery, cost escalation and non-realization of anticipated benefits.
Portfolio reporting	Ensure that the status of each of the top portfolio-level risks is incorporated into the portfolio dashboard and that risk actions are reviewed regularly and updated.

Significantly, the approach was found to identify inconsistencies where dependencies were identified by the 'giving' initiative but not by the 'receiving' initiative. These inconsistencies could therefore be resolved at an early stage. The approach also identified areas where:

▪ Initiatives were claiming to deliver benefits in the same parts of the business – so highlighting areas of potential double counting of benefits.

▪ Benefits forecast from one initiative were based on expansion in one part of the business, whilst other initiatives implied cutbacks in the same part of the business.

Such overlaps and inconsistencies were thus flagged up for further review and amendment to the benefits forecast if required. The approach was used to focus not only on active management of the mission-critical dependencies (including developing appropriate mitigation plans), but also on those initiatives with no identified dependencies, where raising the profile of dependency management will encourage initiatives to re-examine their plans to ensure that there are indeed no dependencies. In a number of instances, dependencies were subsequently identified.

7.6 PORTFOLIO MANAGEMENT PRACTICE 10: STAKEHOLDER ENGAGEMENT

7.6.1 What is the purpose?

The purpose of the stakeholder engagement practice is to provide a coordinated approach to stakeholder engagement and communication and so ensure that:

▪ The needs of the portfolio's customers (both internal and external stakeholders) are identified and managed appropriately.

▪ Stakeholder support for the portfolio is gained by effective consultation and involvement in the definition and delivery of the portfolio.

7.6.2 What is involved?

Effective stakeholder engagement is not simply a 'nice to have' feature. Portfolio management experience in the NPD field has identified the importance of bringing the 'voice of the customer' into the design and development of new products[53] and recent guidance from the UK Cabinet Office[54] has highlighted the role that customer insight and satisfaction measurement can play in ensuring the 'right' programmes and projects are undertaken.

With regard to employees, research for the UK Department for Business Innovation and Skills[55] has found that employee engagement is unequivocally correlated with enhanced competitiveness, profitability and performance. Moreover, improving engagement is linked to improving performance – and the relationship is four times stronger from engagement to performance than vice versa. The report quotes Mandy Symonds of United Welsh Housing Association as saying, 'Being involved not only gives me real opportunities to influence the decisions which affect me and my future, it also means I am more aware of the wider picture.' It is this wider picture that portfolio management is concerned with.

Portfolio-level stakeholder engagement encompasses the following main elements:

■ Management board members being visibly involved and proactively supporting portfolio communications. This helps to embed collaborative working by emphasizing the need to operate as one team.

■ Developing a consistent approach to stakeholder engagement and communications at all levels in the portfolio, ensuring a shared vision of what the portfolio is designed to achieve – and communicating this shared vision effectively.

■ Collaborative working between the portfolio office and the organization's communication experts.

■ The preparation of a portfolio stakeholder engagement and communication plan which should be included in the portfolio management framework. This plan, together with the business change lifecycle, ensures that stakeholders' needs are identified by proactively involving them in the design and development of initiatives, and the decision-making processes where appropriate. In this way, the 'voice of the customer' can be embedded into initiative design and development.

■ The portfolio stakeholder engagement and communication plan being required to identify key stakeholders, categorize them (e.g. by degree of interest and ability to influence a positive outcome) and outline how key messages will be communicated in each case – i.e. the media to be used.

■ Adoption of the champion–challenger model and encouragement of recommendations for process improvement from all stakeholders. In this way, stakeholders can be actively engaged in the portfolio management definition and delivery cycles.

Communication and engagement is not a one-way process from the portfolio office: it is important to ensure that processes facilitate a feedback loop between stakeholders and the portfolio office. This needs to be managed in such a way that stakeholders can see what action has been taken in response to their input.

7.6.3 Focus on senior management

Chapter 4 highlighted that one of the key principles that lays the foundation for effective portfolio management is senior management commitment. The reverse is also true – many failed implementations are attributed to loss of senior management support. The stakeholder engagement and communication plan should therefore include specific focus on building and maintaining senior management commitment. This can be facilitated by:

■ An active board-level portfolio management champion.

■ Engaging with board members both collectively and individually.

■ Providing board members with a briefing based on the executive summary of this guide and supplemented with information from the accompanying publication, *An Executive Guide to Portfolio Management*.

■ Clearly stating what their role is in relation to portfolio management and, specifically, what decisions will be required and when.

■ Communicating a clear and compelling message about 'What's in it for me?'

■ Linking portfolio management and the required behaviours to the performance management processes.

■ Obtaining the support of influential non-executive directors.

Example: Classifying stakeholders

One approach advocated by a US-based professional portfolio practitioner group[56] is to use an organization map to identify and classify key stakeholders as:

- Key thought leaders
- Influencers
- Early adopters
- Potential resistors.

Appropriate strategies can then be developed, including identifying the 'What's in it for me?' (WIIFM) for each group from the implementation of portfolio management.

Example: Stakeholder workshops

There are many perspectives and views on what portfolio management is and should be. One organization ran a number of workshops to help reach a shared vision of what the new organization would look like once portfolio management had been fully implemented. This proved particularly useful not only in enabling all stakeholders to understand where the organization was going (and to contribute to that vision), but also from a team-building perspective because everyone worked collectively and concerns were addressed openly.

7.6.4 Embrace modern communications

In recent years there has been a dramatic increase in the availability of media channels and technology platforms that can be used to enhance portfolio communication – intranet sites, software with centralized forum functionality, messenger technology on laptops and telephones, use of video conferencing, internet meetings, and websites such as Twitter and YouTube are increasingly being used by organizations to enhance their traditional communications. For example:

- Governments worldwide are now using YouTube to communicate directly with the public.
- 20% of the FTSE 100 companies and HM Treasury have a Twitter account.
- Some organizations are starting to integrate audio downloads and videos within their business change lifecycle, so enabling staff to download updates and learn on the move.

It is important that such contemporary technology platforms are not disregarded by the portfolio office, communication or IT departments, who historically might block access to such platforms, as they can usefully augment the more traditional communication channels.

Example: Stakeholder engagement – the Criminal Justice Experience[57]

The 'Criminal Justice Experience' was a one-hour virtual walkthrough of the criminal justice system (CJS) designed to support the CJS IT portfolio by showcasing the end-to-end process, the changes achieved to date and how IT projects and programmes could make a difference to the efficiency and effectiveness of the CJS and impact on front-line staff, victims and witnesses. The objectives of the 'Experience' were defined as follows to:

- Give information in an engaging, modern and believable way.
- Provide a fun/engaging environment to encourage understanding and participation.
- Address public misconceptions about the CJS and increase public confidence so it was seen to be effective.
- Encourage the public to participate in the delivery of justice.
- Help reposition the criminal justice system as a service.

It was targeted at a range of stakeholders including:

- Sponsors (Her Majesty's Treasury, Cabinet Office etc.)
- Delivery partners (CJOs including the police, Crown Prosecution Service, courts, prisons, probation service and youth justice officials – at national and local level)
- Regulators such as the OGC, the NAO and Prime Minister's Delivery Unit
- Opinion formers (media, think tanks etc.).

The 'Experience' commenced with participants watching a short video of a crime. They were then invited to participate by playing the role of key characters – the criminals, the victim and a witness. Participants then physically walked through the system visiting mock points/stages – arrest and charging with the police; building the case with the Crown Prosecution Service; an initial hearing at the magistrates' court; the full hearing at the Crown court; the route of one offender through the youth offending process; and the path of the second adult offender through prison and probation. At each stage the audience received an overview of the processes, the effect on the 'players' (the criminals, the victim and the witness) and the potential of the IT portfolio to make the system more efficient and effective. This was reinforced by the use of visual display boards and presentation material illustrating the process and key benefits. These overviews were presented by trained members of staff acting as narrators at each stage. The Criminal Justice Experience ended with a feedback session where visitors were invited to ask more detailed questions and discuss any issues and thoughts that the 'walkthrough' had stimulated.

More than 1,500 stakeholders including ministers, the media, staff from criminal justice and other organizations, as well as international criminal justice bodies, participated in the tour with satisfaction ratings of more than 90%. Participants were provided with a printed version of the 'Experience' which was also available online.

The 'Experience' was found to deliver a number of key benefits:

■ It helped to raise the profile of the scope of the portfolio with key stakeholders.
■ It facilitated a meaningful, ongoing dialogue between business representatives and the portfolio.

■ It was a very effective way of engaging key stakeholders and providing an end-to-end view of the system.
■ Being held on a fortnightly basis meant that presenters had to stay up to date with progress.
■ It provided a basis for further development and expansion to encompass the wider business reform programme.

7.7 PORTFOLIO MANAGEMENT PRACTICE 11: ORGANIZATIONAL GOVERNANCE

7.7.1 What is the purpose?

The purpose of the organizational governance practice is to ensure clarity about what decisions are made, where and when, and what criteria are used. As discussed in sections 3.7 and 4.4, portfolio management governance should be aligned with the wider organizational governance structure.

7.7.2 What is involved?

The main elements of effective governance of the portfolio include:

■ A vision for what the portfolio is designed to achieve is agreed by the management board and communicated to the organization. This should be documented in the portfolio

Table 7.8 Stakeholder engagement: keys to success

Key	Explanation
Work collaboratively with the organization's communication team	Ensure that the organization's communication team is involved with the creation of the portfolio stakeholder engagement and communication plan.
Involve stakeholders	Make sure that stakeholder needs are understood and that they are actively and regularly involved throughout the portfolio definition and delivery cycles.
Align plans from individual initiatives with the overall portfolio plan	Align the individual stakeholder engagement and communication plans for each initiative with the portfolio stakeholder engagement and communication plan.
Ensure a tailored approach	Stakeholder engagement and communications is a broad and complex subject and requires more than simply 'broadcasting' information to the wider community. Rather, it focuses on tailoring messages and establishing two-way engagement that contributes to portfolio success.
Incorporate a feedback loop	Processes must exist that ensure stakeholders can see how their comments and feedback have been dealt with.
Use contemporary communications	The use of contemporary technology to augment traditional media channels can help engage stakeholders effectively and efficiently.
Focus on senior management	Senior management support is essential to effective implementation of portfolio management and sustaining progress – so pay particular attention to ensuring continued senior management commitment.
Value communication	Communication skills and resources are often not viewed as a priority at the start of the implementation of portfolio management. This is a serious mistake, as without effective communication processes and skills, there is a serious risk of miscommunication, lack of buy-in and the implementation becomes difficult to sustain.

strategy and will need to be updated as the organization's strategic objectives change.

■ A description of what portfolio management is designed to achieve (and the measures used to assess this), and the key processes and governance structures, are included in the portfolio management framework.

■ Role profiles are prepared for key positions, and terms of reference are agreed for the portfolio governance bodies, e.g. portfolio direction group/investment committee and portfolio progress group/change delivery committee (see Appendix B). Role profiles and terms of reference should be included in the portfolio management framework.

■ The business change lifecycle and stage/phase gates are used to ensure that initiatives are appraised, prioritized, approved, monitored and evaluated consistently based on their demonstrable strategic contribution and risk. This governance oversight of initiatives should extend from start gate to post-implementation review.

■ Escalation paths with control/tolerance limits (i.e. where performance deviates beyond a set limit, the matter needs to be referred to the next tier of governance) are clearly defined.

■ The portfolio office is the guardian of the portfolio processes – monitoring their operation, reporting any non-compliance and providing an assurance on their effective operation. This is why the portfolio office should have no direct delivery responsibility, so that they are not seen as being biased in favour of their own operation.

Example: Portfolio governance – NAO

An NAO report[58] shows that effective governance is crucial and highlights a case study from Cambridgeshire County Council, which transformed its governance structures following the introduction of portfolio management. The 'key components' of success were identified as:

■ Securing the support and commitment of senior management to the introduction of portfolio management and the breaking down of existing management structures, so allowing the rapid consolidation of large numbers of disparate projects into smaller more coherent groupings of related programmes.

■ Business cases being kept under review post-approval to ensure that the benefits 'remain relevant and achievable'.

■ Clear and concise information and regular reporting on current status, risks and issues, dependencies, progress against key targets/deliverables and benefits.

■ Support for the process from a corporate project office which was established to bring consistency in project management and delivery and to ensure that scarce resources were 'allocated effectively and efficiently across the portfolio of projects and the authority had the capacity to deliver'.

Table 7.9 Organizational governance: keys to success

Key	Explanation
A shared vision for the portfolio	The management board should agree a vision for the portfolio. This vision should be widely disseminated and should be included in the portfolio strategy and delivery plan as well as the portfolio dashboard report to keep the ultimate objective at the forefront of people's attention.
Clarity about governance	Ensure the governance structures, processes, escalation routes, tolerance/control limits and role descriptions are clearly defined and included in the portfolio management framework.
Regular reviews of business cases and progress	Ensure that the business change lifecycle incorporates regular reviews of continued business justification and strategic alignment – both at the individual initiative level (stage/phase gates) and for the portfolio as a whole.
Shared understanding of the governance structure and processes	Ensure that all key stakeholders have a clear and shared understanding of the governance processes and structure: ■ Make the portfolio management framework widely available via the organization's intranet. ■ The portfolio office should host training and awareness-raising sessions.

Example: Portfolio governance – Peterborough City Council[59]

Portfolio governance at Peterborough City Council consists of:

- Director's group – oversees the corporate programme at a macro level and ensures interaction with the sustainable community strategy. Chaired by the director of resources.
- Governance board – manages all the council's projects and programmes. Decides which projects should go ahead and which shouldn't. Manages the gateway process. Chaired by the head of growth.
- Savings and innovations board – manages the delivery of the transformation projects. 'Calls in' projects where they are in difficulty (red or amber). Coordinates intervention and can cease projects. Chaired by the head of customer services.
- Programme team – reports to the savings board and supports the delivery of all programmes including capital, business as usual and transformation. Led by a senior programme manager.

7.8 PORTFOLIO MANAGEMENT PRACTICE 12: RESOURCE MANAGEMENT

7.8.1 What is the purpose?

At some level the amount of resources available to deliver change initiatives is constrained. The purpose of the resource management practice is to put in place mechanisms to understand and manage the amount of resources available and required and so enable:

- More informed decisions to be made concerning the initiation and scheduling of initiatives to match resource availability.
- More efficient and effective use of available resources – less 'down time', improved balance between internal and external people, and limited resources allocated to initiatives in priority order.
- Improved delivery since initiatives will be less likely to be held up by temporary resource shortages or bottlenecks.
- Improved realization of benefits as the scale and timing of business change required is proactively managed to ensure it is achievable.

7.8.2 What is involved?

Resource management concerns the balancing of demand and supply for any constrained resource that limits the capacity of the organization to deliver its change initiatives. These resources include, but are not limited to, skilled programme and project staff; other specialists; required equipment and accommodation; and the organization's capacity to absorb business change. Here the focus is on managing staff and skills constraints, but the principles apply to managing other limited/constrained resources. The main elements of portfolio resource management are:

- Understand the demand – this requires that consideration be given to the resource requirements including staff and skills (types and timing) of not only the current live programmes and projects, but also those in the development pipeline. This in turn requires that initiatives forecast resource demands accurately and consistently. The portfolio office will therefore need to develop standards for consistent resource forecasting and compile a portfolio resource schedule from the plans of individual initiatives.
- Understand the supply – for example, complete a simple portfolio skills register recording key staff skills, experience and current availability.
- Matching of demand and supply – ensuring the most highly prioritized programmes and projects are first in the queue for limited resources if there is any excess demand. Other factors to be considered include ensuring sufficient contingency and monitoring programme and project delivery, so that slippages are assessed for their impact on the resource schedule and whether additional resources should be bought in. The portfolio office will also be able to predict times when excess supply is forecast and so consider the potential to bring other initiatives forward.
- Gap closure – where shortages in supply (numbers, skills or experience) are forecast, corrective action can be taken in terms of:
  - Planned recruitment.
  - Negotiating contracts with external agencies. Because the portfolio office is clear about the skills required and the timing, it should be possible, in collaboration with HR and procurement, to negotiate improved terms.
  - Staff development.

- Re-scheduling delivery.

Further guidance on resource and capacity management is available in the P3O guide (*Portfolio, Programme and Project Offices*, TSO, 2008).

Example: Resource management

The approach recommended by the US-based Enterprise Portfolio Management Council (EPMC)[60] is as follows.

Demand-side resource management

- Resist trying to control the detail; only model reality as far as is relevant for strategic planning – i.e. at an aggregated level.
- Focus planning and management efforts on large and/or mission-critical projects.
- Group portfolio resources into three categories: skills, facilities and technology environment.

- There are four levers to manage demand for resources:
  - Changing timescales for lower-priority projects to flatten demand.
  - Decouple development from roll-out to help flatten demand.
  - Descope to reduce absolute resources needs.
  - If these are not enough, defer or drop some lower-priority projects.

Supply-side resource management

- Differentiate core competencies from commodity skills.
- Staff/train enough people to cover these core competency needs.
- For commodity skills, develop standard role descriptions, cross-train people and develop good external relationships.

Table 7.10 Resource management: keys to success

Key	Explanation
Set portfolio-wide standards for resource forecasting	Consistent forecasting is essential, so define standards and templates to guide programme and project planners.
Use business cases to create a portfolio resource schedule	Amalgamate the resource plans of the programmes and projects to provide an understanding of the portfolio resource requirements – i.e. what resources (people, skills and capability) are required and for what time periods. Compare this against availability to identify spare capacity and any excess demand.
Review the resource schedule regularly	As initiatives progress, understanding of their resource requirements changes and improves. Consequently the portfolio resource schedule needs to be reviewed and updated on a regular basis – as part of the periodic portfolio-level reviews and at each initiative stage/phase gate at a minimum. Aligning resource management with the business change lifecycle in this way enables more effective resource management and initiative delivery at a portfolio level.
Implement dynamic resource management	Effective resource management is a dynamic process and is often as much art as it is science. Resource forecasts and schedules can help – but they are a guide to effective management rather than fixed plans to monitor against. The portfolio office therefore needs to stay constantly abreast of developments and to consider the implications of changes in the portfolio composition and variances from plan on resource requirements.

Appendix A: Portfolio management health check assessment

A

Appendix A: Portfolio management health check assessment

The following are questions that senior managers are encouraged to ask of themselves and their organizations. This is presented in a format that can aid the preparation of an action plan to guide the adoption of more effective portfolio management.

Key questions	Yes	No	Partly	Action required
1 Do I have a clear view of the current change portfolio?				
▨ What projects and programmes are included?				
▨ What are the predicted costs and benefits at a portfolio level?				
▨ Are the inter-dependencies visible to me, and are we managing them effectively?				
▨ How will this change portfolio impact on the business?				
2 Given our strategic objectives, are all programmes and projects included in the portfolio necessary? And is it clear:				
▨ How each project or programme contributes to our strategic objectives?				
▨ That all funded projects and programmes contribute more than they cost?				
▨ That the selected solutions are being achieved cost-effectively?				
3 When the portfolio and business as usual are looked at together, am I confident that these are the investments that will achieve the organization's strategic objectives?				
4 Are people happy, motivated and driven to successfully implement changes to the organization?				
▨ Do people understand where we are going?				
▨ Do people understand the importance of their role in the journey?				
▨ Do people crave success and work as one portfolio delivery team?				

Continued overleaf

Key questions	Yes	No	Partly	Action required
5 Do I have a clear view of the future change portfolio, including projects in the development pipeline?				
▪ Is the start-up of projects disciplined – i.e. are effective controls in place so that significant resources are only committed to priority projects?				
▪ Are projects progressing through the development pipeline at an acceptable speed?				
6 Project prioritization – do we have a consistent set of metrics for assessing the attractiveness (return) and achievability (risk) of potential investments?				
▪ Do we make collective decisions about the projects and programmes to be included in the portfolio, or is it a situation of 'he/she who shouts loudest'?				
7 In terms of financial management:				
▪ Is the allocation of funds staged and linked to project performance?				
▪ Is a modular approach to project development in place, so that wasted spend is minimized should funding be reallocated?				
8 Are resource demand and supply matched – do we have the right people at the right time with the skills to deliver the portfolio?				
9 Do regular portfolio progress reports provide a clear line of sight on portfolio delivery and impact?				
▪ Do I feel confident that the reported status reflects real status?				
▪ Do I have a clear understanding of the top risks and issues facing the portfolio?				
▪ Are portfolio progress reports the basis for action rather than a template-filling exercise?				
10 Is the return and risk of individual projects actively managed – to increase the former and reduce or mitigate the latter?				
11 Do I clearly understand the portfolio management governance process?				
12 Do I have a clear view of our track record in terms of delivering projects:				
▪ On time?				
▪ To budget?				
▪ To quality?				
▪ With forecast benefits being actually realized in practice?				
13 Am I clear about the difference portfolio management has already made and will make to my organization?				

Appendix B:
Role descriptions

B

Appendix B: Role descriptions

PORTFOLIO DIRECTION GROUP (PDG) OR INVESTMENT COMMITTEE (IC)

Role purpose

This is the governance body where decisions about inclusion of initiatives in the portfolio are made. No initiative should be included within the portfolio or funded without the PDG/IC's approval.

Responsibilities

- Agree the portfolio management framework.
- Agree the processes contained within the portfolio definition cycle and ensure that they operate effectively.
- Approve changes to the practices within the portfolio definition cycle.
- Approve the portfolio strategy and delivery plan.
- Receive investment appraisal and portfolio prioritization reports and decide on the scope and content of the portfolio.
- Ensure that the portfolio is suitably balanced.
- Ensure that resources are allocated appropriately.
- Ensure that the portfolio development pipeline contains sufficient initiatives at the feasibility/concept stage and that initiatives progress through the pipeline at an adequate speed.
- Undertake regular portfolio-level reviews to assess progress and confirm that the portfolio remains on course to deliver the desired strategic benefits and outcomes.
- Review recommendations from the portfolio progress group/change delivery committee and make decisions accordingly.
- Ensure that any conflicts between portfolio delivery and BAU that cannot be resolved by the portfolio progress group/change delivery committee are addressed effectively.
- Promote collaborative working across the organization.
- Undertake periodic reviews of the effectiveness of portfolio management within the organization – and take appropriate action where required.

PORTFOLIO PROGRESS GROUP (PPG) OR CHANGE DELIVERY COMMITTEE (CDC)

Role purpose

This is the governance body responsible for monitoring portfolio progress and resolving issues that may compromise delivery and benefits realization.

Responsibilities

- Agree the processes contained within the portfolio delivery cycle and ensure that they work effectively.
- Approve changes to the practices within the portfolio delivery cycle.
- Ensure that all programmes and projects comply with agreed delivery standards – e.g. use of the business change lifecycle.
- Monitor delivery of the portfolio delivery plan (via the portfolio dashboard) including:
  - Monitor spend against profiled budget and revised forecast outturn:
    - Ensure effective action is taken to address overspends.
    - Where underspends occur, take prompt action to consider reallocating the funds to other initiatives including those in the portfolio development pipeline by referring the issue to the PDG/IC.
  - Review and resolve key portfolio-level issues.
  - Ensure that risks and dependencies are effectively managed.
  - Ensure that limited resources are managed effectively and efficiently.
  - Monitor and approve changes to the benefits forecast.
- Approve communications on portfolio progress.
- Where justified, make recommendations to the PDG/IC for the termination of initiatives.
- Escalate issues that can't be adequately resolved to the PDG/IC and/or management board.
- Undertake periodic reviews of the effectiveness of portfolio delivery within the organization – and take appropriate action where required.

BUSINESS CHANGE DIRECTOR OR PORTFOLIO DIRECTOR

Role purpose

The business change or portfolio director is the management board member who is responsible for the portfolio strategy and provides clear leadership and direction through its life.

Responsibilities

- Champion the implementation of portfolio management across the organization.
- Secure the investment to implement portfolio management, including a portfolio office where required.
- Provide overall direction and leadership for the implementation and delivery of the portfolio.
- Gain relevant management board approval for the portfolio strategy and delivery plan.
- Promote an energized culture that is focused on collaborative working in the interests of the organization as a whole.
- Ensure that the portfolio evolves to reflect changed strategic objectives and business priorities and that resources are reallocated where necessary.
- Ensure that the portfolio management practices are documented in a portfolio management framework and that they are amended in the light of lessons learned.

PORTFOLIO MANAGER

Role purpose

The portfolio manager coordinates the effective and efficient operation of the portfolio management practices and provides support to the business change/portfolio director, portfolio direction group/investment committee and portfolio progress group/change delivery committee – including ensuring that they receive the information they require to enable them to discharge their responsibilities.

Responsibilities

- Drafts the portfolio strategy and delivery plan for the business change/portfolio director.
- Keeps the portfolio management framework up to date.

- Prepares the regular portfolio dashboard for the PDG/IC and PPG/CDC.
- Ensures that business case data (particularly costs, benefits and risks) is prepared on a consistent and reliable basis across the portfolio.
- Undertakes investment appraisals and reports accordingly to the PDG/IC.
- Coordinates portfolio prioritization exercises and reports accordingly to the PDG/IC.
- Ensures that dependencies are effectively managed and where required escalates issues to the PPG/CDC for resolution.
- Leads on the preparation and implementation of the portfolio stakeholder engagement and communication plan.
- Identifies constraints within the portfolio and works to overcome them.
- Identifies improvements to the portfolio management practices, e.g. via membership of appropriate professional groups, post-implementation reviews, submissions under the champion–challenger model, and from periodic portfolio effectiveness and maturity reviews (e.g. those using P3M3 and the health check assessment at Appendix A).

PORTFOLIO BENEFITS MANAGER

Role purpose

The portfolio benefits manager ensures that a consistent 'fit for purpose' approach to benefits management is applied across the portfolio and that benefits realization is optimized from the organization's investment in change.

Responsibilities

- Develops and maintains the organization's portfolio benefits management framework.
- Considers and advises the portfolio manager or director on changes to the portfolio benefits management framework.
- Provides training and awareness-building sessions on the application of the portfolio benefits management framework.
- Participates in investment appraisals, ensuring that business case benefits forecasts are consistent with the organization's benefits eligibility rules.

- Works with the organization's (and programme-based) business change managers to promote more effective benefits management practices.
- Facilitates benefits-mapping workshops.
- Provides advice and support to PPM and BAU colleagues on the development of initiative-level benefits forecasts and benefits management strategies.
- Provides assurance on the effectiveness of benefits management practices at programme and project level.
- Maintains the portfolio-level benefits forecast and ensures that double counting is minimized. Updates the forecast to reflect approved initiative-level changes at stage/phase gates and portfolio-level reviews.
- Coordinates the production of the annual portfolio-level benefits realization plan.
- Consolidates progress reports for the portfolio dashboard and for periodic portfolio-level reviews.
- Escalates any benefits-related issues via the portfolio manager to either the PDG/IC or PPG/CDC.
- Sets the standards for, and monitors, post-implementation reviews to compare benefits realized with benefits forecast and to identify lessons learned in relation to benefits management for wider dissemination.

Appendix C: Programme and project information template

C

Appendix C: Programme and project information template

PURPOSE

The purpose of the programme and project information template is to capture key information regarding current and proposed change initiatives within the organization. Completion of this document forms part of the 'understand' portfolio management practice within the portfolio definition cycle. Using a standard document for all initiatives will help to ensure that consistent information is collected, which helps provide a level playing field for investment appraisals and portfolio prioritization activities.

FITNESS FOR PURPOSE CHECKLIST

- Is the information accurate?
- Have appropriate programme and project managers been consulted and have they agreed the information presented?

SUGGESTED CONTENTS

The programme and project information template should contain the following:

- Programme/project title and ID (completed by the portfolio office)
- Names of key personnel – SRO/sponsor and programme/project manager
- Objectives
- Portfolio category/segment
- Strategic objective contribution
- Outcomes or blueprint contribution
- Key deliverable(s)
- Initial start/finish dates and current lifecycle stage
- Key milestones with planned dates including stage/phase gate reviews
- Cost profile – capital and operating
- Key quantitative benefits (and measures)
- Key qualitative benefits (and metrics to be used to assess progress)
- Risk level – e.g. use of the risk potential assessment (RPA)
- Resource/skills required

- Business changes required
- Key dependencies
- Business as usual area impacted
- Current status/progress to date
- Any other relevant information.

SOURCES OF INFORMATION

Information can be sourced from consultations with programme and project managers and from a review of programme or project documentation including the business case.

Appendix D:
Benefits management
– an example

Appendix D: Benefits management – an example

This appendix contains extracts from Standard Chartered Bank's benefits management guidelines.[61]

BENEFITS CATEGORIES

In order to ensure a consistent approach for calculating benefits cases, the categories below provide the rules for which benefits can be included in the financial business case calculations and which benefits cannot.

The benefits section of business cases should only include tangible financial benefits (commonly referred to as 'hard benefits'), separated into three categories:

- **Incremental revenue** – all types of additional revenue, including where increased volumes and fee margins result in an increased revenue budget or forecast.
- **Cost saves** – all types of cost savings, resulting in a reduction in budgeted and forecast costs as part of the performance management process.
- **Other** – all additional tangible financial benefits resulting in a positive impact to the business's profit and loss accounts, such as balance sheet improvement leading to a proven 'profit and loss' impact.

Furthermore, only tangible financial benefits that meet the following criteria should be included:

- The benefit is realistic, measurable and comparable against a baseline.
- The benefit is included or catered for in a financial budget or forecast and subsequently implemented into business as usual (BAU) activity.
- The benefit is realizable and can be tracked in the general ledger (GL) and/or other financial systems.
- The benefit is 'signed off' by the accountable executive and an appropriate member of the bank's finance community.

Other benefits (commonly referred to as 'soft benefits') that should be documented but not included in the benefits case calculation are:

- Tangible but non-financially quantifiable benefits – these benefits can be measured, but a direct correlation to the impact on the business's 'bottom line' is unable to be made; for example, benefits resulting from improved customer service (and hence expected to protect revenue losses) or improved staff morale.
- Intangible benefits – these benefits cannot be measured and therefore assessed, generally because their magnitude and timing cannot be accurately forecast, such as a positive contribution to the brand or improved decision-making.

BENEFITS CALCULATION RULES

In order to ensure a consistent approach for calculating benefits cases, the following guiding principles should always be followed:

- **Recurring benefit timeframes** – benefits of a recurring nature can be claimed in the first full month that the benefit is realized, not part-way through a month.
- **People cost savings** – benefits associated with headcount savings can only be included where an explicit role (for either a full-time or part-time staff member) is saved and hence there is a cost reduction in a nominated cost centre, even if the resource is deployed elsewhere to fill an organizational 'gap'.
- **Premises cost savings** – benefits associated with premises savings can only be included where a premises saving directly impacting the profit and loss takes place.
- **Revenue protection** – revenue protection should not be included in the financial benefits case, because it is unable to be tracked and validated. However, it should be included when providing a holistic description of the benefits.
- **Cost avoidance** – cost avoidance should not be included in the financial benefits case. However, it should be included when providing a holistic description of the benefits.

IMPORTANCE OF BASELINE DATA

Obtaining appropriate baseline data is critical to demonstrating improvements in performance. The baseline position for tangible financial measures, tangible non-financially quantifiable measures and key performance indicators (KPIs) needs to be identified and agreed at the commencement of a project. This will, as benefits are realized, enable the improvements in performance ('deltas') to be calculated, help validate the assumptions on which the benefits case was based, and aid ongoing tracking and validation during the scheduled periodic and post-implementation reviews.

KPI IDENTIFICATION OVERVIEW

A KPI provides a 'leading' indicator, demonstrating that a change has occurred as forecast by a project. This is particularly useful where non-financially quantifiable benefits are targeted, but is also of value when a number of initiatives contribute to one overall benefit. To measure the varying success and contribution of each initiative, KPIs should be employed to monitor changes in performance at the same time as the realization of the (financial) benefit is tracked.

Where possible, existing KPIs should be used rather than establishing new KPIs. These KPIs should be:

- Simple to understand and communicate to all involved in producing change.
- Specific and detailed – if KPIs are too high-level, it becomes difficult to confirm the cause-and-effect relationship between programme activity and change, as many other influences will come into play.
- Supported by data that is available on a regular basis with limited resource investment.
- Available in a meaningful frequency of measurement.
- Where possible, aligned to individuals' performance objectives.

By monitoring these KPIs over a statistically valid sample size, a clearer understanding of the cause and effect can be established and the improvement in customer satisfaction can be demonstrated.

Illustrative example

Assuming that the targeted objective of a fictitious project is 'to increase the number of customers who are highly satisfied by levels of service in all Hong Kong branches by 30% by the end of Q2', the obvious benefit would be increased customer satisfaction. Given this, the targeted improvement to be monitored through KPIs could be:

Performance improvement	Measure	Frequency	Baseline period	Baseline value
Customer satisfaction	Score (out of 10)	Quarterly	Q4	6.34
Queuing time	Average no. of minutes	Monthly	H2 average	2.15 minutes
Customer complaints	Absolute number	Weekly	Q4 average	26
Closed accounts	% per 10,000 customers	Weekly	Q4 average	0.5%

Appendix E:
Portfolio-level
documentation

E

Appendix E: Portfolio-level documentation

Title	Purpose	Typical contents
Portfolio management framework	To provide all stakeholders with a single, authoritative and up-to-date source of advice on the portfolio management practices adopted by the organization and its governance arrangements.	▪ The objectives of portfolio management. ▪ The investment criteria and portfolio categorization/ segmentation to be used. ▪ The business change lifecycle – timings of stage/phase gates and portfolio-level reviews. ▪ Regular performance reporting and change control. ▪ The governance framework – where, when and by whom key decisions are made and the role of the portfolio office. ▪ Terms of reference for the portfolio boards. ▪ Role descriptions for main portfolio positions. ▪ Overview of the portfolio-level strategies for benefits, finance, risk and resource management and for stakeholder engagement.
Portfolio strategy	To communicate a succinct description of the vision and objectives for the portfolio – and the means by which these objectives will be achieved.	▪ Vision and longer-term objectives for the portfolio endorsed by senior management. ▪ Overview of the strategic priorities. ▪ Top-level information regarding benefits to be realized and how they link to the strategic objectives. ▪ Key strategic risks. ▪ Key dates, measures and success factors. ▪ Key resource and cost information. ▪ Motivational teamwork statement from senior management.
Portfolio delivery plan	To provide a basis for formal senior management approval of planned initiatives and the associated resource requirements. To provide a baseline against which progress will be monitored via the portfolio dashboard.	▪ Shorter-term (often annual) portfolio delivery schedule including key milestones. ▪ Portfolio financial plan – profiled budget by month. ▪ Portfolio benefits realization plan – summary of the benefits to be realized in the year ahead and when. ▪ Key dependencies. ▪ Key risks mitigation action plan. ▪ High-level resource plan/schedule for all limited resources. ▪ Portfolio performance metrics.

Continued overleaf

Title	Purpose	Typical contents
Portfolio benefits management framework	To provide a framework within which consistent approaches to benefits management can be applied across the portfolio.	■ Outline of the high-level benefits the portfolio is designed to achieve and the metrics to be used to assess their realization. ■ Benefits eligibility guidance – the detailed rules on the identification, classification, quantification, valuation and validation of benefits. ■ Treatment of benefits throughout the business change lifecycle – from business case, through stage/phase gates and portfolio-level reviews, to post-implementation review. ■ Definition of roles and responsibilities for benefits forecasting, tracking and reporting.
Portfolio benefits realization plan	To summarize the benefits forecast to be realized in the year ahead and so provide a clear view of the planned returns from the organization's accumulated investment in change. To provide a baseline against which to assess the benefits actually realized.	Statement of the main benefits forecast to be realized in the year ahead including: ■ Scale of impact. ■ Profile throughout the year (when they will be realized – if not monthly then usually at least quarterly). ■ Metrics to be used to assess benefits realization.
Portfolio financial plan	To summarize the financial commitments inherent in the approved portfolio for the year ahead as a basis for formal senior management budgetary approval. To provide a baseline against which to track and compare actual spend.	■ Profiled budget for the year ahead (usually monthly). ■ Analysed separately for capital and operating/resource expenditure.
Portfolio resource schedule	To provide a baseline against which to manage demand and supply for constrained resources.	■ Profiled comparison of demand and supply for constrained resources throughout the planning period, highlighting periods of slack and under-capacity.
Portfolio stakeholder engagement and communication plan	To provide a framework for coordinated and consistent communications across the portfolio.	■ Statement of the objectives of portfolio stakeholder engagement and communications. ■ Description of the key stakeholder groups analysed by interest and influence. ■ Media to be used for each group.
Portfolio dashboard	To provide the portfolio governance bodies with an overview of progress against plan. To identify areas where action is required to address issues impacting, or potentially impacting, on portfolio delivery.	■ Progress information against key milestones. ■ Status on key initiatives, risks, issues and dependencies. ■ Spend and revised forecast compared to the profiled budget. ■ Latest benefits forecast and realization to date compared with plan.

Appendix F:
Assessing the impact of
portfolio management

F

Appendix F: Assessing the impact of portfolio management

Portfolio management can be a source of real value to the organization in terms of:

- Doing the 'right' projects – optimizing the contribution to strategic objectives subject to considerations of risk/achievability.
- Doing projects 'right' – delivery (on time and to budget) and realization of the anticipated benefits.

Achieving this should be more than a leap of faith; a commitment to assessing the impact of portfolio management has several benefits itself:

- It can help to demonstrate a compelling case for investment in portfolio management.
- By helping to identify what's working and what's not working, it helps in the ongoing development of more effective portfolio management practices.
- The process of measurement can help to ensure success – reflecting the management adage, 'what gets measured gets done'.

Measuring success is, however, far from straightforward and consequently it is recommended that a suite of metrics is used to assess progress from more than one perspective, encompassing both quantitative and qualitative data and the dimensions of project and programme delivery on time and to budget; efficient and effective use of constrained resources; strategic coverage and balance; and strategic and operational impact achieved. These can be augmented by a relevant maturity framework such as P3M3. Although the actual metrics used will need to be tailored to the specific circumstances, the following list provides some sample metrics:

- Trend in balance of spend by portfolio category/segment.
- Savings in business case production – cost and time.
- Stage/phase gate and OGC Gateway red, amber, green (RAG) ratings on delivery confidence (see Figure 6.4).
- Post-implementation review ratings for benefits realization against forecast and achievement of value for money (actual benefits compared to actual cost).

- Proportion of initiatives rejected/stopped at each stage/phase gate and portfolio-level review.
- Speed with which initiatives progress through the development pipeline and the shape of this pipeline (it should be a 'funnel' not a 'tunnel').
- Proportion of portfolio in value terms (and by cost) invested in modular programmes and projects.
- Length of projects from inception to closure, e.g. % less than 6 months, 6 months to 1 year, 1 year to 18 months, >18 months.
- Scale (and trend) of reliance on external resources (contractors and consultants).
- Scale of unplanned delays due to resource constraints.
- Scale of unplanned delays due to ineffective dependency management.
- Key resource utilization rates.
- Amount of investment written off.
- Improved reputation for effective change management – assessment by auditors etc.
- Quantitative data on:
  - Percentage of initiatives delivered on time compared with initial forecast.
  - Percentage of initiatives delivered on budget compared with initial forecast.
  - Percentage of benefits realized compared with initial forecast.
- Process maturity assessment – using, for example, the P3M3 model or the health check assessment at Appendix A of this guide.
- Number of portfolio process improvements recommended under the champion–challenger model and from post-implementation reviews.
- Stakeholder survey of views on the efficiency and effectiveness of the portfolio definition practices.
- Stakeholder survey of views on the efficiency and effectiveness of the portfolio delivery practices.

References

References

1 Cabinet Office (2008) Benchmarking Reliable Delivery [unpublished].

2 Cabinet Office (2008) Benchmarking Reliable Delivery [unpublished].

3 Markowitz, H. (1952) Portfolio selection. *Journal of Finance* 7:77–91.

4 Portfolio management definitions developed by the Cabinet Office and OGC.

5 Cabinet Office (2008) Benchmarking Reliable Delivery [unpublished].

6 Jeffery, M. and Leliveld, I. (2004) Best practices in IT portfolio management. *MIT Sloan Management Review*, Spring 2004 Vol. 45 No. 3.

7 Weill, P. and Ross, J. (2004) *IT Governance: How Top Performers Manage IT Decision Rights for Superior Results*, Harvard Business School Publishing.

8 Sharpe, P. and Keelin, T. (1998) How SmithKline Beecham makes better resource-allocation decisions. *Harvard Business Review* March–April 1998.

9 Provided with the kind assistance of Bob Kitchen, Catalyze Ltd.

10 Provided with the kind agreement of Bob Kitchen, Catalyze Ltd.

11 National Audit Office (2006) Delivering successful IT-enabled business change. Available at: www.nao.org.uk/publications/0607/delivering_successful_it-enabl.aspx (last accessed 17.09.10).

12 Best Practices Committee of the Federal CIO Council (2002) Summary of first practices and lessons learned in information technology portfolio management. Available at: www.cio.gov/Documents/BPC_portfolio_final.pdf (last accessed 17.09.10).

13 Provided with the kind assistance of Paul Hirst, HMRC.

14 Heskett, J. L., Sasser, E.W. Jr. and Schlesinger, L. A. (1997) *The Service Profit Chain: how leading companies link profit and growth to loyalty, satisfaction, and value*. New York: The Free Press.

15 Heintzman, R. and Marson, B. (2005) People, service and trust: is there a public sector service value chain? *International Review of Administrative Sciences*, 71: 549.

16 The contribution of Dr Peter Bevan of Queensland University of Technology, in bringing the empirical research to the attention of the authors, is gratefully acknowledged.

17 Guidance on decision-conferencing is available from Phillips, L.D. and Bana e Costa, C.A. Transparent prioritization, budgeting and resource allocation with multi-criteria decision analysis and decision-conferencing. *Ann Oper Res* (2007) 154:54–68. Published online: 17 May 2007 Springer Science+Business Media, LLC 2007.

18 Provided with the kind agreement of Paul Hirst, HMRC.

19 Provided with the kind agreement of Bob Kitchen, Catalyze Ltd.

20 Detailed examples of a P3O vision and blueprint can be found in OGC's P3O guidance.

21 HP case study in Sanwal, A. (2007) *Optimizing Corporate Portfolio Management*, Wiley.

22 Morris, S. (2007) Organisational Energy in the NHS.

23 Bruch, H. and Ghoshal, S. (2003) Unleashing organizational energy. *Sloan Management Review*, Vol. 44, pp. 45–51; and Bruch, H. and Vogel, B. (2011) *Fully Charged: how great leaders boost their organization's energy and ignite high performance*, Harvard Business Review Press, Boston.

24 Bruch, H. and Vogel, B. (2011) *Fully Charged: how great leaders boost their organization's energy and ignite high performance*, Harvard Business Review Press, Boston.

25 Shaw, P. (2006) *The Four V's of Leadership: vision, values, value added, vitality*, Wiley.

26 Reinsvold, C., Johnson, E. and Menke, M. (2008) Seeing the forest as well as the trees: creating value with portfolio optimization. *SPE* 116419.

27 See Ward, J. and Daniel, E. (2006) *Benefits Management – delivering value from IS & IT Investments*, Wiley.

28 Source: IT Governance Institute. ©2009 ITGI. All rights reserved. Used by permission.

29 See www.hm-treasury.gov.uk/data_greenbook_guidance.htm.

30 See the HMT *Green Book* coverage of optimism bias at www.hm-treasury.gov.uk/data_greenbook_supguidance.htm.

31 See www.communities.gov.uk/publications/corporate/multicriteriaanalysismanual.

32 See www.ogc.gov.uk/documents/Prioritisation_Categories.pdf.

33 See www.ogc.gov.uk/introduction_to_the_resource_toolkit_tools_techniques.asp.

34 For more information see Using the analytic hierarchy process to improve enterprise portfolio management, by James Devlin in Levine, H.A. (2005) *Project Portfolio Management*, Jossey Bass.

35 Provided with the kind assistance of Paul Hirst, HMRC.

36 Source: IT Governance Institute. ©2009 ITGI. All rights reserved. Used by permission.

37 Provided with the kind assistance of Bob Kitchen, Catalyze Ltd.

38 Provided with the kind assistance of Bob Kitchen, Catalyze Ltd.

39 Provided with the kind assistance of Rob Parker and Ian Barnard, Pcubed.

40 Provided with the kind assistance of Paul Hirst, HMRC.

41 In the UK central government the five-case framework (Strategic, Economic, Financial, Commercial and Management) is recommended by HM Treasury and the OGC. See www.hm-treasury.gov.uk/data_greenbook_business.htm.

42 Sanwal, A. (2007) *Optimising Corporate Portfolio Management*, Wiley.

43 See www.best-management-practice.com.

44 National Audit Office (2008) *Managing Financial Resources to Deliver Better Public Services*. Available at: www.nao.org.uk/publications/0708/managing_financial_resources_t.aspx (last accessed: 17.09.10).

45 See www.best-management-practice.com.

46 Provided with the kind assistance of David Palmer, Home Office.

47 Provided with the kind assistance of Heather Darwin, Peterborough City Council.

48 See the HMT *Green Book* Annex 4; Lovallo, D. and Kahneman, D. (2003) Delusions of success – how optimism undermines executives' decisions. *Harvard Business Review*, July 2003, pp56–63; and Flyvbjerg et al. (2003) *Megaprojects and Risk*, Cambridge University Press.

49 Provided with the kind assistance of Heather Darwin, Peterborough City Council.

50 See www.ogc.gov.uk/guidance_management_of_risk.asp.

51 See www.hm-treasury.gov.uk/d/orange_book.pdf.

52 Pennypacker, J. and Retna, S. (eds) (2009) *Project Portfolio Management – a view from the management trenches*, Wiley.

53 See, for example, Cooper, R.G. and Edgett, S.J. (2007) *Generating Breakthrough New Product Ideas*, PDI.

54 For example, see www.cse.cabinetoffice.gov.uk/UserFiles/File/Customer_Insight_Primer.pdf and www.cabinetoffice.gov.uk/media/cabinetoffice/corp/assets/publications/delivery_council/pdf/emerging_principles.pdf.

55 Engaging for success: enhancing performance through employee engagement. Available at http://www.nhsemployers.org/SiteCollectionDocuments/Macleod%20Review.pdf (last accessed 10.10.10).

56 Pennypacker, J. and Retna, S. (eds) (2009) *Project Portfolio Management – a view from the management trenches*, Wiley.

57 Jenner, S. (2009) *Realising Benefits from Government ICT Investment – a fool's errand?* Academic Publishing.

58 National Audit Office (2006) Delivering successful IT-enabled business change. Available at: www.nao.org.uk/publications/0607/delivering_successful_it-enabl.aspx (last accessed 17.09.10).

59 Provided with the kind assistance of Heather Darwin, Peterborough City Council.

60 Pennypacker, J. and Retna, S. (eds) (2009) *Project Portfolio Management – a view from the management trenches*, Wiley.

61 Provided with the kind agreement of Tim Carroll, Standard Chartered Bank.

62 Adapted from the definition at www.businessdictionary.com/definition/strategic-objective.html.

Glossary

Glossary

aggregated risk

The overall level of risk to the portfolio when all the risks are viewed as a totality rather than individually. This could include the outputs of particular scenarios or risk combinations.

assurance

All the systematic actions necessary to provide confidence that the target (system, process, organization, programme, project, outcome, benefit, capability, product output, deliverable) is appropriate. Appropriateness might be defined subjectively or objectively in different circumstances. The implication is that assurance will have a level of independence from that which is being assured.

benefit

The measurable improvement resulting from an outcome perceived as an advantage by one or more stakeholders.

business as usual (BAU)

The way the business normally achieves its objectives.

business change lifecycle

A generic name used to represent any organizational process or framework which helps to guide the delivery of programmes and projects using a collection of repeatable processes and decision points.

categorization

Splitting a portfolio into organizationally appropriate categories or segments – for example, by initiative type or investment objective. The organization's investment criteria can be tailored to suit each category of investment.

centre of excellence (CoE)

A coordinating function ensuring that change initiatives are delivered consistently and well, through standard processes and competent staff. It may provide standards, consistency of methods and processes, knowledge management, assurance and training. It may also provide strategic oversight, scrutiny and challenge across an organization's portfolio of programmes and projects. It may be a function within the wider scope of a portfolio office. This function provides a focal point for driving the implementation of improvements to increase the organization's capability and capacity in programme and project delivery.

champion–challenger model

A technique whereby everyone is expected to comply with the defined portfolio processes (the current 'champion') but anyone can recommend a change (a 'challenger'). Once adopted, the 'challenger' becomes the new 'champion' process. Such challengers should be encouraged as a way of ensuring engagement across the organization, and the number of submissions received should be monitored on a regular basis.

clear line of sight

A technique that seeks to ensure a transparent chain from strategic intent through to benefits realization.

decision-conferencing

A technique whereby managers consider and debate in a facilitated workshop the relative weightings to attach to the organization's strategic objectives; the criteria to be used to assess strategic contribution in each case; and the scores to allocate to individual initiatives. In this way the portfolio governance body comes to a collective decision on the composition of the portfolio. This has been found to be very effective in terms of optimizing portfolio returns and also results in enhanced commitment to the portfolio and to the portfolio management processes.

design authority

A role or function (permanent, temporary or virtual) that provides expert specialist advice or owns some organizational function, service, standard or strategy that will be affected, or a major programme outcome or change that needs to be controlled. This could be an IT or property infrastructure design, or a major service contract; it could also be a business process model or the programme blueprint or corporate target operating model. The design authority provides expertise and guidance on a specific area to ensure that there is appropriate alignment and control when changes are being planned and implemented. At a programme level this role may advise or own the business blueprint management on behalf of the programme manager. At the enterprise level, this role may manage the enterprise architecture of the organization.

development pipeline

The initiatives under development, concept and feasibility testing, prior to formal inclusion in the portfolio as 'live' programmes and projects.

end project report

A report given by the project manager to the project board that confirms the handover of all products and provides an updated business case and an assessment of how well the project has performed against its project initiation documentation.

gated review

A structured review of a project, programme or portfolio as part of formal governance arrangements carried out at key decision points in the lifecycle to ensure that the decision to invest as per agreed business cases and plans remains valid.

governance (portfolio)

Encompasses the structures, accountabilities and policies, standards and processes for decision-making within an organization in order to answer the key strategic questions 'Are we doing the right things?', 'Are we doing them the right way?' and 'Are we realizing the benefits?'

health check

A health check is a quality tool that provides a snapshot of the status of a project, programme or portfolio. The purpose of a health check is to gain an objective assessment of how well the project, programme or portfolio is performing relative to its objectives and any relevant processes or standards. A health check differs from a gated review in that it is a tool used for assurance purposes by the portfolio office to inform specific actions or capability maturity development plans, whereas a gated review is part of formal governance arrangements.

hurdle rate of return

The target rate of return set by an organization, which potential investments need to achieve in order to be considered for funding. Also used as the discount rate to convert future cash flows into the net present value.

initiative (change initiative)

A programme or project.

management board

Generic term used to describe either a project management board, programme management board or portfolio management board, or any combination based on the MoP context.

management by exception

A technique by which variances from plan that exceed a pre-set control limit are escalated for action – for example, where spends exceed budget by 10%.

Managing Successful Programmes (MSP)

An OGC publication/method representing proven programme management good practice in successfully delivering transformational change, drawn from the experiences of both public and private-sector organizations.

one version of the truth

A technique whereby each element of portfolio progress reporting (costs, benefits, progress etc.) is derived from an agreed source managed by the portfolio office. Individual initiatives and other organizational functions will provide data inputs in relation to cost, benefit, delivery progress, resource requirements, dependency and risk status – and to an agreed schedule. The resulting consolidated data will be recognized as the authoritative source of information on portfolio progress used for monitoring, reporting and management decision-making.

optimism bias

Defined by the HM Treasury *Green Book* as the demonstrated systematic tendency for appraisers to be over-optimistic about key project parameters, including capital costs, operating costs, works duration and benefits delivery. To address this, adjustments should be made to the estimates of programme and project costs, benefits and works duration based on empirical data. Standard adjustments are included in the HMT *Green Book* and on the HMT website.

organizational energy

The extent to which an organization (division or team) has mobilized its emotional, cognitive and behavioural potential to pursue its goals.

P3M3

The portfolio, programme and project management maturity model, which provides a framework with which organizations can assess their current performance and put in place improvement plans.

Pareto rule

Also known as the '80:20 rule' which states that 80% of gains will come from 20% of study activity.

PESTLE

Acronym for 'political, economic, social, technological, legal and environmental'. A technique used generally in organizational change management to undertake an environmental scan at a strategic level.

pet project

A project that is championed by an executive in an organization that may be aligned to an individual goal or goals for a specific part of the business, but not necessarily aligned to the strategic imperatives of the organization as a whole.

portfolio

The totality of an organization's investment (or segment thereof) in the changes required to achieve its strategic objectives.

portfolio dashboard

A technique to represent decision support information at an amalgamated level using tabular and graphical representation such as graphs and traffic lights.

portfolio definition cycle

One of the two continuous cycles within the portfolio management model containing portfolio management practices related to defining a portfolio, i.e. understand, categorize, prioritize, balance and plan.

portfolio delivery cycle

One of the two continuous cycles within the portfolio management model containing portfolio management practices related to delivering a portfolio, i.e. management control, benefits management, financial management, risk management, organizational governance, stakeholder engagement, and resource management.

portfolio delivery plan

A collection of tactical information regarding the planned delivery of the portfolio based on the overarching portfolio strategy. The portfolio delivery plan usually focuses on the forthcoming year in detail in terms of schedule, resource plans, costs, risks and benefits to be realized.

portfolio management

Portfolio management is a coordinated collection of strategic processes and decisions that together enable the most effective balance of organizational change and business as usual.

portfolio management framework

The central repository containing a description of the agreed portfolio management practices adopted by the organization and its governance arrangements.

portfolio management model

A logical diagram describing the relationship between the portfolio management principles, cycles and practices.

portfolio office

An office which is established centrally to manage the investment process, strategic alignment, prioritization and selection, progress tracking and monitoring, optimization and benefits achieved by an organization's projects and programmes on behalf of its senior management.

portfolio principles

The portfolio management principles represent the foundations upon which effective portfolio management is built – by providing the organizational culture and environment in which the portfolio definition and delivery practices can operate effectively. They are senior management commitment; alignment with organizational strategy; alignment with the organizational governance framework; a portfolio office; and an energized change culture. These are generic principles – the way in which they are applied should be tailored to suit the organizational circumstances so long as the underlying rationale is maintained.

Portfolio, Programme and Project Offices (P3O)

The decision-enabling and support business model for all business change within an organization. This will include single or multiple physical or virtual structures, i.e. offices (permanent and/ or temporary), providing a mix of central and localized functions and services, and integration with governance arrangements and the wider business such as other corporate support functions.

portfolio strategy

A collection of top-level strategic information that provides total clarity to all stakeholders regarding the content and long-term objectives of the portfolio. The portfolio strategy is an important communication tool and as such should be motivational to the reader.

PRINCE2

A method that supports some selected aspects of project management. The acronym stands for PRojects IN Controlled Environments.

reference class forecasting

A technique where forecasts of an initiative's duration, costs and benefits are derived from what actually occurred in a reference class of similar projects. Alternatively, estimates can be built up in the traditional manner and then adjusted by set percentages based on past performance – this is the approach used in the UK central government where a standard set of optimism bias adjustments are included in the HMT *Green Book*.

resource

An organization's physical or virtual entities (human or otherwise) that are of limited availability and can be used to undertake operations or business change.

senior responsible owner (SRO)

The single individual with overall responsibility for ensuring that a project or programme meets its objectives and delivers the projected benefits.

stage/phase gate review

Structured reviews of a project, programme or portfolio as part of formal governance arrangements that are carried out at key decision points in the lifecycle to ensure that the decision to invest as per agreed business cases and plans remains valid.

start gate

A stage/phase gate review which applies at the early stages of the policy-to-delivery lifecycle. It offers departments the opportunity to gain independent assurance on how well practical delivery issues are being addressed in preparing for implementation.

strategic objectives[62]

The measurable outcomes that demonstrate progress in relation to organization's mission and to which the portfolio should contribute. According to Peter Drucker they fall into eight types:

- Market standing: desired share of the present and new markets
- Innovation: development of new goods and services, and of skills and methods required to supply them
- Human resources: selection and development of employees
- Financial resources: identification of the sources of capital and their use
- Physical resources: equipment and facilities and their use
- Productivity: efficient use of the resources relative to the output
- Social responsibility: awareness and responsiveness to the effects on the wider community of the stakeholders
- Profit requirements: achievement of measurable financial well-being and growth.

strategy

The approach or line to take, designed to achieve a long-term aim. Strategies can exist at different levels in an organization – in *Managing Successful Programmes* there are corporate strategies for achieving objectives that will give rise to programmes. Programmes then develop strategies aligned with these corporate objectives against particular delivery areas.

SWOT analysis

Acronym for 'strengths, weaknesses, opportunities and threats'. A technique to determine favourable and unfavourable factors in relation to business change or current state.

three-point estimating

A technique whereby project estimates are prepared on three bases: best-case scenario; worst case; and most likely. Estimates can then be calculated by multiplying the most likely estimate by 4, adding the best and worst case estimates, and dividing the total by 6.

zero-based budgeting

A technique for determining the next period's budget, whereby rather than adjusting the previous year's funding, all material activities are examined to justify the scale of funding for each, 'bottom-up' from a zero-base.

Index

Index